For

3 May 1982

TROLLOPE
AND HIS
ILLUSTRATORS

Also by N. John Hall

THE TROLLOPE CRITICS (*editor*)

TROLLOPE
AND HIS
ILLUSTRATORS

N. John Hall

St. Martin's Press
New York

Library of Congress Cataloging in Publication Data

Hall, N. John
    Trollope and his illustrators
    Includes bibliographical references and index.
    1. Trollope, Anthony, 1815–1882—Illustrations.
    2. Illustration of books—Great Britain. 3. Millais,
    John Everett, Sir, bart., 1829–1896. I. Title.
    PR5685.5.H3 1979   823'.8   79–476
    ISBN 0–312–81888–2

CONTENTS

LIST OF PLATES

These plates reproduce the originals in their actual size, except where dimensions are given (in inches, height preceding width).

J. E. MILLAIS

vii

74. 'And why does he come here?' *He Knew He Was Right*
75. Monkhams. *He Knew He Was Right*
76. Aunt Stanbury at dinner will not speak. *He Knew He Was Right*
77. 'I wonder why people make these reports.' *He Knew He Was Right*
78. Four vignettes. Capitals for Chapters vii, x, xiii and xlvii. *He Knew He Was Right*

F. A. FRASER

79. 'It's dogged as does it.' *The Last Chronicle of Barset*

F. HOLL

80. Lady Laura at the Glass. *Phineas Redux*
81. Original wash drawing for 'Lady Laura at the Glass'. $6\frac{1}{4} \times 4\frac{1}{4}$.

ARTIST AND ENGRAVER

82. Wood block for 'Lord Lufton and Lucy Robarts'
83. J. E. Millais. Pen-and-ink and grey wash drawing. $6 \times 5\frac{1}{4}$

ACKNOWLEDGEMENTS

The plates are reproduced by courtesy of the following: the Robert H. Taylor Collection, Princeton University Library (plates 1, 3, 5, 6, 8–11, 13–21, 23–5, 27, 28, 30, 36, 44–6, 48, 51–78 and 80); the Arents Collection, New York Public Library (plate 2); Thos. Agnew & Sons, Ltd (plate 4); the Morris L. Parrish Collection, Princeton University Library (plate 7); The Hartley Collection, Museum of Fine Arts, Boston (plates 12, 22, 81 and 82); a private collection in New York (plates 26, 31–3, 35, 37–42, 47, 49, 50 and 79); Orley Farm School, Harrow (plate 29); the Victoria and Albert Museum (plate 34); a private collection (plate 43); a private collection in London (plate 83).

PREFACE

The volume of critical attention devoted to the fiction of Anthony Trollope has only just begun to extend to the illustrations that accompanied his novels on their first appearance. Moreover, through the years, writers on English book illustration have contented themselves with glowing but brief comments on the drawings by Trollope's principal illustrator, John Everett Millais. In this study I shall supply bibliographical and biographical data about the work of Millais and other artists for Trollope and hazard some judgments on the merits of the drawings as illustrations to the novels. To art historians I leave the inviting subject of a closer examination of the drawings as drawings.

Almost inevitably, all illustrations for Victorian novels come to be measured against those for Dickens' novels. This is unfortunate. The work of Browne and Cruikshank for Dickens and that of the Sixties artists who illustrated Trollope differ so radically in style that it is positively futile to argue superiority. But it is worthwhile to note here one very relevant difference between the illustrations for Dickens and Trollope: while the Dickens illustrations have been reproduced so often that for many, as for the young Henry James, *Oliver Twist*, for example, seemed 'more Cruikshank's than Dickens's', the Trollope illustrations are for the most part unfamiliar. They have remained the province of antiquarian book collectors and students of Sixties illustration. One of the contributions of this book is to make available reproductions of many of the original plates. My concern has been with original illustrations only, i.e. those published under Trollope's aegis and which found their way into first or very early English book editions. The authority invested by Trollope himself in these illustrations and, in many cases, their incontestable excellence as drawings, dictated this decision.

Fifteen Trollope novels were illustrated in their original magazine-serial or part-publication, and these contained more than 300 full-page illustrations (and 100 quarter-page vignettes), most of which were included in the first book editions. Because of the unmanageably large number of illustrations and their very uneven quality, I have had to select for reproduction only the most representative. In the interest of comparison I have, however, included a handful of unsuccessful illustrations; I have necessarily referred to others in the text. While no one will complain of the exclusion of the drawings by later and inferior artists, some will regret the absence of about half the Millais illustrations; but because Millais supplied eighty-six drawings for Trollope, a selection even in his case was necessary. When—if ever—a complete scholarly edition of Trollope's novels is published, it certainly ought to reproduce the original illustrations. In the meantime this book will place before Trollope's readers many of the best of them.

The following persons have given me valuable assistance and suggestions: Ruth apRoberts, Nina Burgis, Robert S. Call, Nancy M. Coffin, M. A. Ford, Mortimer Frank, Theodore Grieder, John Halperin, E. D. H. Johnson, Thomas Lange, Allan R. Life, Daniel Lowenthal, J. S. Maas, Michael Mason, Mario Materassi, William E. Miller, Gabriel M. Naughton, Karin Peltz, Sarah Phelps, Gordon N. Ray, Robert H. Taylor, Alexander D. Wainwright, Malcolm Warner, Bernard Witlieb, Andrew Wright, and my wife Marianne.

Parts of the discussion of Millais were published in somewhat different form as 'Millais' Illustrations for Trollope', University of Pennsylvania *Library Chonicle*, 42 (Summer 1977) and are reprinted with permission.

I acknowledge gratefully a fellowship from the National Endowment for the Humanities.

New York, 1979   N.J.H.

INTRODUCTION

The case against the illustration of fiction has taken various forms. Du Maurier's *Trilby*, a novel more frequently praised for its drawings than its writing, and one in which, since author was also illustrator, a close if not perfect harmony between picture and text could be expected, drew this comment from Henry James:

> In going over *Trilby* in the first English edition, the three volumes from which the illustrations were excluded, I have found it a positive comfort to be left alone with the text; and quite in spite of my fully recognizing all that, in the particular conditions, was done for it by the pictures and all that it did in turn for these. I fear I can solve the riddle only by some confession of general jealousy of any pictorial aid rendered to fiction from outside; jealousy on behalf of a form prized precisely because, so much more than any other, it can get on by itself.[1]

James advances his objections somewhat tentatively and almost apologetically, as if his were a minority view. The modern reader quite often resents any non-verbal representation in fiction: he desires nothing to interpose itself between his imagination and the writer's; he finds illustration distracting, limiting, inhibiting—a positive disservice. Furthermore, many critics are convinced that illustration itself is a hybrid art, a compromised or dependent form and as such generally inferior. Both artists and public, it is said, share this view of the illustrator as a second-class artist.

On the other hand, the apologist for illustrated fiction begins by asserting that he, along with many readers, past and present, sophisticated or not, finds illustration for particular novels a positive assistance and enrichment. He suggests that opera and ballet, though 'mixed' arts, are not for that reason held in disrespect, and he laments rather than denies the prejudice against the illustrator as first-rate artist. If pressed about the calibre of such artists, he resorts, in the case of the English artists, to the mention of Hogarth, Rowlandson, Blake, and Turner, although as regards illustrated fiction he would do better to name

Cruikshank, Browne, and Millais. But to say this is really not to meet the issues. Moreover, persons with radical objections to illustrated fiction will not be won over by argument; theirs is a preference to be respected. More fruitful discussion must come from proponents of illustration, particularly with regard to its province and function in the novel. That the number of authors whose fiction appeared successfully illustrated on first publication is distinctly small, and limited in English literature to a handful of Victorian authors, is generally admitted. Furthermore, since the illustration of adult fiction, long out of style (except perhaps in a minor way on some dust jackets), seems unlikely to be revived, the number of successfully illustrated original novels is apparently quite fixed. A related question is the advisability of furnishing established fiction with new illustrations. One of the few modern advocates of the practice, Lynton Lamb, an illustrator himself—he has in fact illustrated Trollope—admits that some works of imagination are 'closed to *any* kind of illustration'.[2] But his qualified approval of latter-day illustration is in keeping with his defence of the autonomy of the artist, whom he would grant the prerogative of choosing and interpreting the subject without any suggestion from the author. Here Lamb's position seems wrongheaded. Certainly the present investigation into the original illustrations for Trollope is largely predicated upon the undeniable authority Trollope gave them: in many cases he selected the subject for illustration and, of Millais' work at least, voiced his very generous approval. The original plates were an integral part of the book, one may say of the text, on its first appearance.

Beyond the consideration of the legitimacy and province of illustration, there remain the crucial questions of the relationship between text and illustration and the specific function of illustration for fiction. Two recent studies, both in connection with Dickens, offer very acceptable general statements. J. Hillis Miller writes:

> The relation between text and illustration is clearly reciprocal. Each refers to the other. Each illustrates the other, in a continual back and forth movement which is incarnated in the experience of the reader as his eyes move from words to picture and back again, juxtaposing the two in a mutual establishment of meaning. . . . Such an intrinsic relation between text and picture sets up an oscillation or shimmering of meaning in which neither element can be said to be prior. The pictures are about the text; the text is about the pictures.[3]

And Q. D. Leavis says that successful illustrations are

> a unique addition to the text, not only visualizing a scene for us in its historical social detail, and giving a visual embodiment to the characters which expresses their inner selves for us inescapably, besides being a visual embodiment of dramatic flash-points: the illustrations are frequently indispensable even to us, the highly-trained modern reader, in interpreting the novels correctly because they encapsule the themes and give us the means of knowing with certainty where Dickens meant the stress to fall.[4]

To examine this reciprocity of text and illustration and the extent to which the Millais illustrations (any discussion of Trollope's illustrators is inevitably one of Millais 'and others') fulfil these functions will be the burden of this study. For it is only in regard to 'visualizing a scene for us in its historical social detail' that agreement is nearly universal: if Trollope is the recognised chronicler of his age, the 'Voice of an Epoch', Millais is readily conceded a similar place among illustrators for his accurate pictorialisation of the details of Victorian life, from dress and posture to the interiors and furnishings of homes. What James said of Du Maurier applies as well to Millais:

> He has reproduced every possible situation that is likely to be encountered in the English novel of manners; he has interpreted pictorially innumerable flirtations, wooings, philanderings, ruptures. The interest of the English novel of manners is frequently the interest of the usual; the situations presented to the artist are apt to lack superficial strangeness. A lady and gentleman sitting in a drawing-room, a lady and a gentleman going out to a walk, a sad young woman watching at a sick-bed, a handsome young man lighting a cigarette—this is the range of incident through which the designer is called upon to move. But in these drawing-room and flower-garden episodes the artist is thoroughly at home; he accepts of course the material that is given him, but we fancy him much more easily representing quiet, harmonious things than depicting deeds of violence.[5]

In so far as the illustrations supply this kind of socio-historical detail they are of more help to the modern reader than they were to his Victorian counterpart. In any case they complement the text in that they accomplish pictorially what Trollope did not choose to do with words, for Trollope's fiction is frequently short on physical description but long on dialogue and analysis of characters' thoughts or feelings. On this one point alone, then, one can make a good case for the illustrations to Trollope's fiction. Their success at providing visualisations of inner selves of characters, highlighting dramatic points, expressing themes, and supplying emphasis, will emerge as individual novels are examined.

That many Victorian novels were illustrated in their first appearance was due almost entirely to the success of Dickens' *Pickwick Papers*. The vogue of illustrated fiction was tied closely to the practice of publishing novels in monthly parts or serially in magazines, for these formats usually called for illustration as a component of the marketing effort. It was not customary, however, to illustrate a novel when published in the three-volume form prevalent in the nineteenth century.[6] Frequently, when a novel made its mark and went into later editions, illustrations would be added, as though only proven sales could justify the expense.

Part-issue was at least a century old before the appearance in 1836 of *Pickwick* in shilling numbers, but the format had not been used for original fiction. The reason lay largely with the stamp tax, which would have rendered far too dear a form of publication meant to be inexpensive. Part-issue or 'number' publication was used most often for cheap reprints, and for inexpensive editions of the Bible or lengthy histories. A most attractive feature of part-issue was the accompanying plate or plates. Indeed, in series such as William Combe's *Dr Syntax's Tours* (1812–21) and Pierce Egan's *Life in London* (1821–8), letterpress was decidedly subordinated to the illustrations, and it was in fact this kind of picture book that Chapman & Hall intended when they asked the young Charles Dickens to supply the narrative for a series of sketches of sporting life by the artist Robert Seymour. The story of the phenomenal success of *Pickwick Papers* is among the most celebrated in English literary history. One factor was economic: here was a work, not only longer than the average three-decker novel, but with the extra attraction of many illustrations, and it could be purchased piecemeal for a shilling a month. Even when added up, the total cost of the nineteen issues (the last being a double number), which had been spread over almost two years, came to but one pound, and the subsequent bound edition sold for only twenty-one shillings. This outlay was considerably less than the standard three-decker price of 31s. 6d. As Richard Altick says, 'Now English readers began to resume the habit of buying books rather than borrowing.'[7] But what need concern us here is that suddenly the most popular novelist in England was issuing his fiction in shilling numbers of which illustrations were an integral part. (After Seymour's suicide, Dickens reduced the number of illustrations per number from four to two and thus set a lasting precedent of issuing two plates per part.) Almost overnight, illustrated fiction became popular.

Dickens contributed still further to the prominence of illustrated fiction with his next work, *Oliver Twist*, which appeared serially in *Bentley's Miscellany* (1837–9). Again, novel-length original fiction had not often appeared in magazines. Smollett, as editor of the *British Magazine*, had published therein his own *The Adventures of Sir Launcelot Greaves* (1760–1); but this was an isolated instance until a handful of novels were serialised in the 1830s, chiefly those by Captain Marryat in his own *Metropolitan Magazine*.[8] But *Oliver Twist* bestowed Dickens' prestige and popularity on the magazine publication of novels, and of course *Oliver Twist*, like *Pickwick*, was illustrated.

Thus part-issue of the novel, and, to a less extent, magazine serialisation of the novel, owed their popularity to Dickens. Other writers, notably Ainsworth, Lever, Mrs Trollope, Surtees, Thackeray, and later Trollope himself, took up publication in parts, and their works so issued were invariably illustrated. Novels appearing serially in magazines were illustrated or not, according to the general practice of the publication in question, but Dickens had opened the way here as well as in shilling-part publication.

Dickens was also instrumental in changing the very size and format of original book editions of many nineteenth-century novels. For while the standard three-volume post-octavo format at a guinea and a half continued to be popular, it was seriously challenged by the one- or two-volume larger demy octavos bound from shilling parts or sheets. And of course all these latter books included the illustrations that had originally appeared in the shilling part. Dickens published ten novels in this new demy-octavo illustrated format; as Kathleen Tillotson remarks, 'it was natural that Dickens should retain this pattern of publication as a kind of trade-mark'.[9] Trollope eventually published eleven illustrated novels in the newer demy-octavo size. *Framley Parsonage*, like *Oliver Twist*, was unusual in that when the text was reset for book publication after magazine serialisation, it was done in the three-volume post-octavo format, with the result that the illustrations were a trifle too large for the page.

By happy accident most of Trollope's illustrated fiction, and much of his very best work, was produced during that remarkable period of English black-and-white illustration, the 1860s. For if, as is generally conceded, these years were the 'golden decade' of reproductive wood engraving, they were also the years when Trollope's popularity made him, as one reviewer remarked, 'almost a national institution'. Of Sixties illustration so much of a general nature has been written that it is sufficient to draw attention to the standard authorities. Most important, despite their rather too impressionistic approach, are two long studies, Gleeson White's *English Illustration: 'The Sixties'* (1897) and Forrest Reid's *Illustrators of the Sixties* (1928). White's huge catalogue was the pioneer work; looking back on the 1860s, it demanded the status of art for the popular product of illustrator and engraver and deemed that decade a flowering comparable to the blossoming of English part music in the Elizabethan age. Reid's still more elaborate study placed greater stress on the variety of work produced and saw the period more in terms of a 'movement'. But the two are seldom far apart. White, for example, says: 'There can be little doubt that the pre-Raphaelites gave the first direct impulse to the newer school. . . . But for "the sixties" proper, the paramount influence was Millais—the Millais after the pre-Raphaelite Brotherhood was disbanded.'[10] Reid in a parallel passage writes: 'though the Pre-Raphaelites did much to influence, and prepare the way for, the later men, the artistic movement associated with the sixties is by no means a Pre-Raphaelite one.'[11] A varying judgment on Millais made for the difference of emphasis here, for although Reid admired Millais' work, he was unwilling to admit that Millais 'occupies quite the position in relation to his fellow-illustrators allotted to him by Gleeson White, as a kind of demi-god among mortals'.[12] Other commentators have elaborated upon points made by White and Reid. Basil Gray, for example, took up Reid's idea of a 'movement' and saw the Sixties as 'the greatest achievement of the English print', and as an 'attempt—which nearly succeeded' in its effort to 'popularize art'. He ascribed the failure to the lack of interest or defection on the part of the Pre-Raphaelites.[13] A more recent writer, Percy Muir, sees the Sixties chiefly in terms of the great wood engravers, especially the Dalziel brothers. Muir's stress upon the wood engraver is well taken, although he overstates his point when he claims that the 'real hall-mark' of a Sixties book consists in its having been 'commissioned by the engraver and executed by him'.[14] The Dalziels did, in effect, publish books over the imprint of such publishers as Routledge, who contributed little more than distribution facilities. But the Dalziels and other engraving firms executed innumerable commissions for publishers of illustrated books and magazines, and part-issue serialisations of fiction. On the other hand, Muir's emphasis can serve to remind one of the gradual displacement of metal engraving and etching by wood engraving. The triumph of wood engraving, of course, did not occur suddenly in 1860, or in 1855, the year of Allingham's *Music Master*, a work illustrated by Rossetti, Millais and Hughes and often spoken of as the first Sixties book. No one accepts dates for artistic periods as definitive, but since Dickens' last novel to be illustrated with Browne's etchings was *A Tale of Two Cities* in 1859, and since Trollope's first illustrated fiction was wood-engraved in 1860, the student of the novel may be tempted to see the change as rather abrupt. The fact is that after Thomas Bewick had introduced—or reintroduced—wood engraving in England about the turn of the century, the new medium had gradually taken over. As early as the 1850s wood engraving had largely supplanted metal engraving and etching in book and magazine illustration, in the latter category most notably in *Punch* and the *Illustrated London News*, founded in 1841 and 1842 respectively. By the 1860s wood engraving completely dominated the field, not only in the popular press but in 'fine art' books as well.

It is impossible to offer an acceptable definition of Sixties style, but one is perhaps safe in characterising it as strongly influenced by the Pre-Raphaelite insistence on a return to nature and careful attention to detail. Whatever their differences, various Sixties artists had in common a strongly representational style. They were not caricaturists, and herein lay a greater difference from the earlier school than that between wood engraving and etching. Millais drew the human figures of his illustrations from the life and 'took flying visits to the country' for his backgrounds,[15] practices entirely foreign to Browne or Cruikshank.[16] But for Sixties artists, aside from this 'naturalistic' tendency and a somewhat literal rendering of the subject, stylistic divergencies were such as to make generalisation difficult. Somehow the 'movement' attracted into the popular market the very best of English artists, men as different as Rossetti, Sandys, Hughes, Du Maurier, Houghton, Mahoney, Walker, Pinwell, Foster, Solomon and North. And Trollope was very fortunate, as he was the first to admit, in that for four novels and two frontispieces his illustrator was Millais, one of the foremost Sixties artists.

JOHN EVERETT MILLAIS

John Everett Millais began to illustrate Trollope's first serialised novel in 1860. The artist at the time was only thirty, but those years had been crowded with great promise, controversy and achievement. Although he would work productively until 1896 when he was to die famous, wealthy, and President of the Royal Academy, most modern critics consider the years after 1860 to have been anticlimactic. The first three decades of his life, however, are a biographer's delight. A child prodigy, Millais at nine had won a silver medal from the Society of Arts; at eleven he entered the Royal Academy Schools, the youngest student ever admitted; at fourteen he won the medal for drawing from the antique; at eighteen he took the Gold Medal for oil painting. Then in 1848, the year of revolutions, Millais, together with Holman Hunt and D. G. Rossetti, founded the Pre-Raphaelite Brotherhood, and although the Brotherhood as such was short-lived, Pre-Raphaelite influence dominated British art for the next fifty years and has inspired more comment than any similar phenomenon in British art history. Millais' Pre-Raphaelite period, which produced such celebrated and controversial paintings as *Christ in the House of His Parents*, *Mariana*, *Ophelia*, and *Autumn Leaves*, lasted until about 1860. Rossetti in 1853 thought that Millais' election as an Associate of the Royal Academy signalled the end: 'So now', he wrote, 'the whole round table is dissolved.'[1]

But Millais continued in his Pre-Raphaelite style. Ruskin—even after the terrible rending that culminated in 1855 when Millais married Effie Gray after her marriage to Ruskin had been annulled—could in his *Academy Notes* be most generous to Millais in 1856.[2] In the following year, however, the sentimentalism of Millais' *Sir Isumbras at the Ford* provoked general derisive outcry; the loosening of technique brought on Ruskin's pronouncement, 'not merely Fall—it is Catastrophe'. In 1859, for different reasons, *The Vale of Rest*—'those terrible nuns', as *Punch* called the painting—roused more critical attack. 'The fact of the matter is,' Millais wrote to his wife, 'I am out of fashion.'[3] But with *The Black Brunswicker*, exhibited in 1860, Millais gained new confidence. The public was enthusiastic about the picture, his friends encouraged him, and he took little heed of the luke-warm press reports. Twentieth-century critics have thought of Millais after 1860 as an apostate from the high aims of art who indulged the British public with sentimental, anecdotal paintings and conventional, if workmanlike, portraits and landscapes.[4] The received explanation, and it has much truth in it, holds that Millais looked upon his art too much as a means of making a living and supporting his family (he was to have eight children). Millais himself is said to have admitted at an exhibition of his collected works in 1886 his failure to fulfil the promise of his youth. At the time, not many in Britain were of this mind. But dissent from the general praise heaped upon Millais was voiced in a work called *Letters to Living Artists* (1892). The anonymous critic spoke of the 'pot boiler canvasses' of the 'spoiled genius' who smothered the 'soul of a great master in the body of a Philistine Briton', the artist who 'left art and theory for the gross reality of worldly success . . . a robust Esau who under stress of motives obvious even though insufficient, was willing to sell his birthright for a mess of pottage'. The anonymous author of these invectives was in fact Gleeson White, and part of his anger was occasioned by Millais' indiscriminate praise of the black-and-white work appearing in *Punch*, the *Graphic*, and the *Illustrated London News* in the 1880s. White called it an 'immeasurably saddening revelation that you, the draughtsman of the *Cornhill* in its golden days, the artist of the ''Twelve Parables'' and many another masterpiece of English woodcutting at its zenith, should by implication place a lower, and as we now view it, a decadent stage of the art, above that of its most splendid founder'.[5] The splendid founder, in White's eyes, was of course Millais himself. And a very convincing case can be made that Millais' ten years of black-and-white work, beginning with William Allingham's *Music Master* in 1855, and including the Moxon *Tennyson* in 1857, the famous *Parables of Our Lord*, together with his illustrations for Sixties periodicals such as *Once A Week*, and, to be sure, his illustrations for Trollope, represent an accomplishment superior to anything he ever did other than the celebrated Pre-Raphaelite oils of the 1850s.

Framley Parsonage

The collaboration of Trollope and Millais arose out of the circumstances attendant upon Trollope's first appearance in serial fiction, the publication of *Framley Parsonage* in the *Cornhill Magazine*. *Framley Parsonage* was the novel that made Trollope truly popular and started him on his career as the king of serial novelists; it also gave his financial fortunes a substantial boost and facilitated his introduction into literary London. Prior to 1860 Trollope had published eight novels. The first three had been failures, but after the appearance of *The Warden* in 1855 his reputation had slowly grown, although he had as yet no great popularity. The highest sum a novel of his had commanded from a publisher was £400. Moreover, because he had spent most of his productive years in Ireland, Trollope was an outsider to the literary life of the capital. But from Ireland, on 23 October 1859, he wrote to Thackeray, editor of the soon-to-be-published *Cornhill Magazine*, and asked to be included as a contributor. Trollope proposed that Thackeray accept every other month—alternating with *Harper's Magazine*—one of his 'Tales of All Countries'. To Trollope's delight he received a reply from George Smith, publisher and owner of the *Cornhill*, offering him £1000 for a three-volume novel to be serialised in the new venture. Two days later, Thackeray, in a gracious letter, welcomed Trollope to the *Cornhill*, complimenting him on his work, telling of his own special delight in *The Three Clerks*, and hoping for 'as pleasant a story' for the magazine.[6] Trollope readily accepted, troubled as he was about getting the first part of his story into Smith's hands by 12 December. The honour, the connection with Thackeray (whom he had long idolised but never met), the money, all seemed more than he had dared to hope for. But what surprised Trollope most was that the *Cornhill* had still at this late hour to provide itself with a full-length novel. Trollope, in his usual self-depreciating way, wrote,

> Thackeray had himself intended to begin with one of his own great novels, but had put it off till it was too late . . . . *Lovel the Widower* was not substantial enough to appear as the principal joint at the banquet. Though your guests will undoubtedly dine off the little delicacies you provide for them, there must be a heavy saddle of mutton among the viands prepared. I was the saddle of mutton. . . . My fitness lay in my capacity for quick roasting.[7]

Trollope hurried to London and spoke to Edward Chapman for whom he had contracted to write (and had one third finished) a novel of Irish life called *Castle Richmond*. Chapman graciously released him from the agreement, but Smith wanted no Irish story, and suggested, Trollope tells us, 'the Church, as though it were my peculiar subject. . . . He wanted an English tale, on English life, with a clerical flavour.'[8] Trollope began the new story on his way back to Ireland, and *Framley Parsonage* took pride of place on the first page of the first issue of the spectacularly successful *Cornhill*. But with all the hurry on everyone's part, no illustrations attended *Framley Parsonage*, although the *Cornhill* was to pride itself on illustrations and although Thackeray's own *Lovel the Widower* had one full-page illustration plus a vignette, both his own drawing.[9] Smith set about getting an illustrator for *Framley Parsonage* and asked Trollope to select a subject from the third instalment. Trollope replied:

> I think the scene most suited to an illustration in part 3 of Framley parsonage would be a little interview between Lord Boanerges and Miss Dunstable. The lord is teaching the lady the philosophy of soap bubbles, and the lady is quoting to the lord certain popular verses of a virtuous nature. The lord should be made very old, & the lady not very young. I am afraid the artist would have to take the description of the lady from another novel I wrote, called Dr Thorne.
>
> As this occurred to me I mention it, but I still leave the matter to your better judgement,—or to anyone else who may have a better judgement.[10]

The letter reveals a number of attitudes in which Trollope remained constant: he wanted literally accurate illustrations; he sought consistency in the depiction of characters he would carry over from one novel to another; and, while he preferred to choose the subjects for illustration, he was willing to grant his artist the final word.

As it happened, the first illustration for *Framley Parsonage* appeared not in the third but in the fourth instalment, probably because of Millais' difficulty in meeting the earlier deadline rather than a disinclination for the subject Trollope had selected. In the meantime Smith hinted to Trollope that he was negotiating with Millais—to which Trollope ecstatically responded, 'Should I live to see my story illustrated by Millais no body would be able to hold me.'[11] By this time Trollope had attended the first 'Cornhill Dinner' and had been introduced to many leading

Lord Lufton and Lucy Robarts.

1. J. E. Millais. *Framley Parsonage*

2. Original pencil drawing for 'Lord Lufton and Lucy Robarts'

literary and artistic figures, Millais among them. One wonders if Trollope had forgotten his own snide remark in *The Warden* about the villainous Tom Towers adorning his quarters with a painting by Millais of a 'devotional lady looking intently at a lily as no lady ever looked before' (Chapter xiv; actually, Trollope's description fits Charles Collins' *Convent Thoughts* more than anything by Millais).[12]

Millais' first drawing for Trollope was 'Lord Lufton and Lucy Robarts' (plate 1). For Lufton, Millais had very little description to follow, except that the young lord was 'a fine, bright-looking young man; not so tall as Mark Robarts, and with perhaps less intelligence marked on his face; but his features were finer, and there was in his countenance a thorough appearance of good-humour and sweet temper' (Chapter ix). Of Lucy we are told only that she was nearly nineteen, clever yet retiring, small in stature and dark in complexion—one of the 'little brown girls' Trollope was so fond of. In Millais' drawing the two had just met for the first time, and Lord Lufton, a brace of pheasants over his shoulder, is leaving her at the parsonage gate. Millais, using the wicket gate to frame the pair, drew a tall, self-assured, aristocratic young man and a tiny, shy young woman. Millais idyllicised the first Trollope illustration, partly by adding a pair of doves to the background. As the collaboration between Millais and Trollope proceeded, only occasionally did Millais depart from more 'realistic' interpretations.

We do not know what Trollope thought either of Millais' choice of subject or of his rendering of it. Presumably, he was pleased. But difficulty arose over the second illustration. Here, Millais again chose the subject; in a letter to his wife on 3 May 1860, he wrote: 'I must now go and read *Framley Parsonage*, and try and get something out of it for my drawing.'[13] He decided upon a scene from the end of Chapter xvi where Lucy, having foolishly told Lufton that she could not love him, goes to her room and throws herself upon her bed. Trollope, told of Millais' choice, was asked to provide the caption. He determined upon 'Was it not a lie?'. 'The above', he wrote, 'taking the words from the text, is I should say the best legend for the picture. I am glad that Millais found a subject in Chap. 16, but the plate will illustrate the last line in the volume!'[14] But when Trollope saw the drawing in proof, he wrote angrily to Smith:

I can hardly tell you what my feeling is about the illustration to the June N° of F. parsonage. It would be much better to omit it altogether if it be still possible,—tho I fear it is not—as the copies will have been

14

sent out. The picture is simply ludicrous, & will be thought by most people to have been made so intentionally. It is such a burlesque on such a situation as might do for Punch, only that the execution is too bad to have passed muster for that publication.

I presume the fact to be that Mr Millais has not time to devote to these illustrations, & if so, will it not be better to give them up? In the present instance I certainly think that you & Mr Thackeray & I have ground for complaint. . . . Even the face does not at all tell the story, for she seems to be sleeping. I wish it could be omitted.[15]

Opinion has long been divided on the merits of 'Was it not a lie?' (plate 3). Bradford Booth, for example, annotated Trollope's letter with the remark that the Millais illustration '. . . *is* very bad. Lucy, who has thrown herself on the bed, weeping, is wearing a dress with an enormous bustle and spreading flounces that makes her look very like a peacock.' On the other hand, Gleeson White used this drawing to exemplify the superiority of Sixties illustrators over their predecessors: 'So long as Thackeray's drawing of *Amelia* is accepted as a type of grace and beauty, how can the believer realise the beauty of Millais's *Was it not a lie?* . . . in the one there is real flesh and blood, real passion, real art, in the other a merely conventional symbol.'[16] And Joseph Pennell singled out this plate as 'splendid'.[17] Two contemporary notices of the novel commented on the drawing: 'J.A.' in *Sharpe's London Magazine* wrote in a hostile review that if one accepted as definition of the novel something representing 'solely the *manners* of the time in which it is written', then *Framley Parsonage* would be a 'model novel'. He added:

Surely, Mr. Millais, when he drew that personification of crinoline representing Lucy Robarts in a state of woe, was in an humour of grim satire. There could not be a better emblem of the book than this picture. The pretty woeful face and clasped hands and little pendant foot (though this must be booted in a horse-breaker fashion) squeezed into odd corners to give due prominence to that mountain of flounces, are as the touches of real human nature which Mr. Trollope has sparsely scattered on the outskirts of his huge mass of conventionalism.[18]

The drawing then is good but for the wrong reasons. An unidentified writer for the *Saturday Review* had a remarkably similar observation, although his notice, for all its condescension, was on the whole more favourable to the book:

15

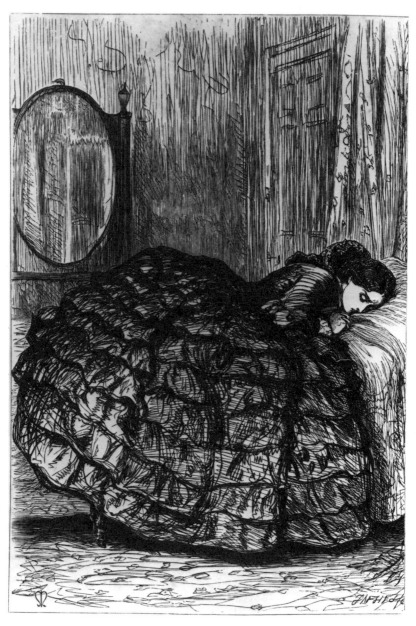

Was it not a he?"

3. J. E. Millais. *Framley Parsonage*

4. Pen-and-ink and watercolour, 'Was it not a lie?'

The best idea of Mr. Anthony Trollope's book is suggested by the skill of the artist who has illustrated it. Opposite the last page of the first volume is to be seen a picture by a well-known hand, the talent of which cannot be disputed. The subject of the plate is Lucy Robarts' crinoline, and the reader's eye following the folds of the crinoline, will come at last upon Lucy Robarts' face and shoulders, which have retired into a corner of the picture, in concession to the social claims of muslin and of lace. The expression on the heroine's handsome face is indicative of despair. She has lost her lover, as she believes, and has flung herself down to indulge her heart in its natural girlish grief. In the foreground the artist has placed one of the heroine's boots. In the background may be seen an oval mirror. The tableau is in all respects worthy of the novel. Mr. Millais, in a congenial moment of social inspiration, has been so fortunate as to hit off in this one illustration the whole spirit of the book. None of Mr. Trollope's figures in their wildest grief could be drawn except in their every-day dress.[19]

Both writers agree that the dress rather than Lucy is the subject of the drawing, and both, though for different reasons, acknowledge the appropriateness of the illustration. Whatever one thinks of these criticisms, one can be fairly certain that if the illustration seems to contain a touch of caricature, it is only because Millais has so literally rendered the crinoline and flounces of the day. This last-mentioned fact, and Millais' next illustration two months later, soothed Trollope:

Many thanks [Trollope wrote to Smith] for the Magazine. The Crawley family is very good, and I will now consent to forget the flounced dress. I saw the *very pattern of that dress* some time after the picture came out.[20]

The drawing that so pleased Trollope included Millais' interpretation of Josiah Crawley, who six years later would reappear in *The Last Chronicle of Barset* and whose superb characterisation has given to that novel first ranking among Trollope's forty-seven novels. In *Framley Parsonage*, Trollope, after relating briefly the unhappy history of Crawley's fifteen years as an impoverished, debt-ridden clergyman, describes him thus:

[Crawley] was a lean, slim, meagre man, with shoulders slightly curved, and pale, lank, long locks of ragged hair; his forehead was high, but his

The Crawley Family.

5. J. E. Millais. *Framley Parsonage*

face was narrow; his small grey eyes were deeply sunken in his head, his nose was well-formed, his lips thin, and his mouth expressive. Nobody could look at him without seeing that there was a purpose and a meaning in his countenance. He always wore, in summer and winter, a long, dusky grey coat, which buttoned close up to his neck and descended almost to his heels. He was full six feet high, but being so slight in build, he looked as though he were taller. (Chapter xv)

Millais has done his homework, for this description from an earlier chapter is perfectly embodied in 'The Crawley Family' (plate 5). But if Crawley himself is well drawn, the children are much less so. On the other hand, the drawing is a good example of Millais' gift for composition: the Crawley family, six in all, is neatly grouped into a triangle at the right, balanced by Lucy, entering from the left.

'The Crawley Family', like 'Lord Lufton and Lucy Robarts', serves chiefly to introduce the characters, for the tableau-like drawing has no particular dramatic interest. Lucy's entrance is not essential to the narrative implications of the illustration, although her service to the Crawley family will contribute towards Lady Lufton's eventual acceptance of her as daughter-in-law. Far more important to furthering the story is the next illustration, 'Lady Lufton and the Duke of Omnium' (plate 6); it is also the first instance in which a subject of Trollope's choice was drawn:

There is a scene [Trollope wrote to Smith] which would do well for an illustration. It is a meeting between Lady Lufton & the Duke of Omnium at the top of Miss Dunstable's staircase. . . . If Mr Millais would look at it I think he would find that it would answer. If so I would send him the vol. of Dr Thorne in which there is a personal description of The Duke of O.[21]

Millais seems to have followed Trollope's suggestion about consulting *Doctor Thorne*. Of the Duke there is no description in *Framley Parsonage*, whereas in *Doctor Thorne* we are told that he was a 'plain tall man' who could be gracious or coldly silent as he chose; of Miss Dunstable we read in *Framley Parsonage* only that she was, according to Mark Robarts, 'neither young, nor beautiful, nor peculiarly ladylike'. In contrast to this vagueness, the description in the earlier novel is specific:

In age she was about thirty; but Frank [Gresham] . . . put her down as being ten years older. She had a very high colour, very red cheeks, a large mouth, big white teeth, a broad nose, and bright, small, black eyes. Her hair also was black and bright, but very crisp and strong, and was combed close round her face in small crisp black ringlets. (Chapter xvi)

In Millais' illustration, we see her, ringlets and all, a few fictional years later, bringing together Lady Lufton and the Duke of Omnium.

Trollope had prepared assiduously for the meeting of Lady Lufton and the Duke, this confrontation of Tory and Whig, of East and West Barsetshire, of moral fastidiousness and laxity, proper widow and profligate bachelor. Much of the novel turns on the confrontation of the two worlds personified by Lady Lufton and the old Duke: the main plot is Mark Robarts' involvement with the latter world and its hangers-on, while owing allegiance to the former. Thus we hear frequently Lady Lufton's opinion of the Duke; in Chapter v, for example, Trollope writes:

It was so thoroughly understood at Framley Court that the duke and all belonging to him was noxious and damnable. He was a Whig, he was a bachelor, he was a gambler, he was immoral in every way, he was a man of no Church principle, a corrupter of youth, a sworn foe of young wives, a swallower up of small men's patrimonies; a man whom mothers feared for their sons, and sisters for their brothers; and worse again, whom fathers had cause to fear for their daughters, and brothers for their sisters;—a man who, with his belongings, dwelt, and must dwell, poles asunder from Lady Lufton and her belongings!

In the chapter describing the meeting of the two protagonists, Trollope makes further good use of his mock-heroic style:

Miss Dunstable had been fully aware of the impropriety of bringing Lady Lufton and the Duke of Omnium into the same house at the same time. . . . But now all things were going wrong, and Lady Lufton would find herself in close contiguity to the nearest representative of Satanic agency, which, according to her ideas, was allowed to walk this nether English world of ours. Would she scream? or indignantly retreat out of the house?—or would she proudly raise her head, and with

Lady Lufton and the Duke of Omnium

6. J. E. Millais. *Framley Parsonage*

outstretched hand and audible voice boldly defy the devil and all his works?

The actual encounter, occasioned by the Duke's brushing accidentally against Lady Lufton's dress, is carefully detailed:

[Lady Lufton] turned round quickly, but still with much feminine dignity, removing her dress from the contact. In doing this she was brought absolutely face to face with the duke, so that each could not but look full at the other. 'I beg your pardon,' said the duke. They were the only words that had ever passed between them, nor have they spoken to each other since; but simple as they were, accompanied by the little by-play of the speakers, they gave rise to a considerable amount of ferment in the fashionable world. Lady Lufton, as she retreated back ... curtseyed low; she curtseyed low and slowly, and with a haughty arrangement of her drapery that was all her own; but the curtsey, though it was eloquent, did not say half so much,—did not reprobate the habitual iniquities of the duke with a voice nearly as potent, as that which was expressed in the gradual fall of her eye and the gradual pressure of her lips. When she commenced her curtsey she was looking full in her foe's face. By the time that she had completed it her eyes were turned upon the ground, but there was an ineffable amount of scorn expressed in the lines of her mouth. (Chapter xxix)

Of this kind of little comic drama Trollope was absolute master, and a close examination of the drawing shows how Millais caught it in detail and spirit. Lady Lufton is arranging her dress, her curtsey is indeed slow and dignified, her eyes appear to have closed themselves against the iniquity before her. The Duke, bowing slightly, looks directly at her. Particularly effective is the empty space between the two—all eyes are upon this central spot in the drawing. Even the chandelier above points to it, and it is in this vacuum that the drama takes place. The illustration does more than capture a particular moment in the narrative and show 'what the characters really looked like' at the time. To be sure, Millais has done this and very delightfully. But his illustration also serves to encapsulate a particular theme of the novel. Trollope himself approved the drawing in proof: 'Many thanks', he wrote Smith, 'for the copy of Millais' illustration which I like very much. The scene makes a better picture than the ladies bustle—however I shall not mean to say a word more about that.'[22]

Mrs Gresham and Miss Dunstable.

7. J. E. Millais. *Framley Parsonage*

"Mark," she said, "the men are here."

8. J. E. Millais. *Framley Parsonage*

Millais supplied two more illustrations for the novel, 'Mrs. Gresham and Miss Dunstable' (plate 7) and '''Mark,'' she said, ''the men are here''' (plate 8), the latter notable in that the face of Mark Robarts is more individualised than any other in the book. These drawings are typical of many illustrations for Trollope in depicting but two characters and typical also of Millais' rendering in that, as in the drawing of Mrs Gresham and Miss Dunstable, one of the characters is seen from the back. Moreover, the two plates demonstrate Trollope's (or Millais') habit in his selection of subjects of alternating seemingly insignificant moments with important ones; here the first is decidedly less dramatic than the second.

Framley Parsonage, published in sixteen instalments in the *Cornhill* from January 1860 to April 1861, was illustrated at somewhat irregular intervals. The explanation may have been economy on Smith's part, or Millais' crowded schedule. Six plates are certainly enough to 'illustrate' a novel (whether a single plate, usually a frontispiece, does so is debatable), but that number was far below what was customary in illustrated Victorian fiction. It is curious, for example, that Mark Robarts, the nominal hero of the book, is not depicted until the last plate. And equally remarkable is the omission of any drawing of Nathaniel Sowerby, the 'villain' of the story.

After the success of *Framley Parsonage* Trollope continued to publish his fiction serially, whether illustrated or not. Thus, of the thirty-nine novels Trollope produced from 1860, only five were originally released in book form, usually in extraordinary circumstances. *Castle Richmond* (1860) had been promised to Chapman & Hall; *Rachel Ray* (1863), originally commissioned for appearance in *Good Words*, was turned down for reasons of 'morality';[23] the serial rights for *Ayala's Angel* (1881) were purchased but never exercised by the National Press Agency; *An Old Man's Love* (1884) was published posthumously. Thus, after 1860, only *Miss Mackenzie* (1865) appears to have been written without serial publication in mind. Of the eight novels published serially in parts, all but one, *The Prime Minister*, were illustrated; of the twenty-six novels to appear first in magazines, eight were illustrated, nine if one counts *Kept in the Dark*, which had a single illustration. (*The Struggles of Brown, Jones, and Robinson*, published without illustrations in the *Cornhill*, 1861–2, had four undistinguished plates by an unidentified hand in its first English book edition, 1870.) That some magazine serials were not illustrated followed from the standing policy of the publication: for example, *Blackwood's* and *All the Year Round* never used illustration.

Orley Farm

Before *Framley Parsonage* had completed its run in the *Cornhill*, Trollope made his first appearance in the monthly shilling part, over the imprint of Chapman & Hall, the publishers who had brought out *Pickwick* in this form in 1836. *Orley Farm* was published from March 1861 to October 1862 and contained forty full-page illustrations by Millais. Trollope wrote: 'I am proud of *Orley Farm*;—and am especially proud of its illustrations by Millais, which are the best I have seen in any novel in any language.'[24] For his personal library, Trollope commissioned a half morocco binding for a set of artist's proofs of the *Orley Farm* illustrations, for which he supplied captions and identifications. At the beginning of the album he inscribed:

> I have never known a set of illustrations so carefully true, as are these, to the conception of the writer of the book illustrated. I say that as a writer. As a lover of Art I will add that I know no book graced with more exquisite pictures. A.T.[25]

Trollope was no flatterer, even of his best friends, among whom Millais came to hold a special place, and if it is an exaggeration to call the illustrations for *Orley Farm* 'the best . . . in any novel in any language', it would not be rash to call them the best for an English novel of the 'golden decade' of wood engraving.

No evidence survives as to whether Trollope chose the subjects for illustration in *Orley Farm*, but it seems unlikely that he would not have done so at least tentatively, as he had for the novels immediately preceding and following this one. Of the forty illustrations, twenty-four touch 'the great Orley Farm case', most of them dealing with Lady Mason's struggles with her adversaries, her loved ones, and herself. Of the concomitant love stories, especially the Felix Graham–Madeline Staveley match, there are fourteen illustrations, and of the comic relief sub-plot of the Moulder–Kantwise group, two illustrations. But *Orley Farm* is clearly Lady Mason's story, and it was natural that she should figure most prominently in the illustrations. Indeed one can trace her sad career closely through Millais' plates.

The first illustration of Lady Mason, 'There was sorrow in her heart, and deep thought in her mind' (plate 9), shows her alone, brooding. She has just spoken to Sir Peregrine Orme of the possible renewal by her enemies

" There was sorrow in her heart, and deep thought in her mind."

9. J. E. Millais. *Orley Farm*

of the Orley Farm litigation, and he, while promising to stand by her, has dismissed her fears as groundless. Lady Mason, left alone, realises how far off the mark Orme has been, for twenty years earlier she had in fact forged the codicil to her late husband's will in order that her son might inherit Orley Farm. At this point the reader can only suspect the forgery, but her gloom foreshadows its eventual revelation. Millais' drawing uses the sunlight streaming in from the verandah door very effectively—she herself is half in light and half in shadow, very much her condition. What the world and her friends know and what she knows are as different as light and dark. She is similarly seated with her face half lighted as Sir Peregrine's grandson (also ignorant of her guilt) tells her she would 'injure' Sir Peregrine by marrying him, 'Peregrine's Eloquence' (plate 10).

In the next illustration of Lady Mason, 'Guilty' (plate 12), she has thrown herself at Sir Peregrine's feet and wrapped her arms around his knees. In one sense the episode is the climax of the novel, for by her confession she is not only admitting her guilt to her benefactor but abandoning all hope of marriage to him. Trollope, in the *Autobiography*, acknowledged the error of placing this event at mid-point in the story. But as one does not read Trollope for intricate plot construction or the unravelling of mysteries, Trollope's assessment may be inapposite. At any rate, he seems to have thought this his best single episode; he ventured to bracket it with great scenes from Scott, Charlotte Brontë, and Thackeray.[26]

In Millais' drawing Sir Peregrine stands stiffly upright, his right arm and hand outstretched almost as if to ward off her words. He is very much the focus of the illustration; Lady Mason abases herself before him, and it is on him that our eye fastens. Her gesture, however genuine, is melodramatic, but the superb rendering of Sir Peregrine, with his mingled shock, dismay, and sympathy, while he maintains his composure, turns what could have been a disaster into a successful illustration.[27] Just as 'Guilty' rescues its subject from melodrama, the very next illustration, 'Lady Mason after her Confession' (plate 13), illuminates and exalts its text. Trollope, in describing Lady Mason as she walks from her interview with Orme, resorts to rather strained language and a litany of cliché:

> ... she felt that all of evil, all of punishment that she had ever anticipated, had now fallen upon her. There are periods in the lives of some of us ... when ... we call on the mountains to fall and crush us, and on the earth to gape open and take us in. When, with an agony of intensity, we wish that our mothers had been barren. ... There was her

Peregrine's Eloquence.

10. J. E. Millais. *Orley Farm*

11. Touched proof, 'Peregrine's Eloquence'

Guilty.

12. J. E. Millais. *Orley Farm*

Lady Mason after her Confession

13. J. E. Millais. *Orley Farm*

Lady Mason going before the Magistrates.

14. J. E. Millais. *Orley Farm*

The Court.

15. J. E. Millais. *Orley Farm*

Lady Mason leaving the Court.

16. J. E. Millais. *Orley Farm*

Bridget Bolster in Court.

17. J. E. Millais. *Orley Farm*

Farewell!

18. J. E. Millais. *Orley Farm*

Farewell !

19. J. E. Millais. *Orley Farm*

burden, and she must bear it to the end. There was the bed which she had made for herself, and she must lie upon it. No escape was possible to her. She had herself mixed the cup, and she must now drink of it to the dregs. (Chapter xlv)

In the next paragraph, Trollope, returning to his customary simple prose, tells of her sitting upon the unmade bed in her room, wrapped in a shawl against the cold. 'She was numbed, and, as it were, half dead in all her limbs, but she had ceased to shake as she sat there, and her mind had gone back to the misery of her position.' Here Millais has collaborated perfectly. The figure of Lady Mason is totally in dark against the austere and almost completely white background of the room. Her head and shoulders are bowed, but not excessively; one lock of hair is displaced on her forehead; her right hand is almost clenched. Millais shows her making no effort to seem anything other than that which she feels herself to be.

After these climactic developments interest shifts largely to the legal manoeuvrings and courtroom scenes of her case (Trollope had an almost obsessive interest in all aspects of the law). In 'Lady Mason going before the Magistrates' (plate 14) Millais has daringly drawn her coming straight at the reader in long, dark, spreading crinoline; her hands in a muff, her face veiled, she is a dark pyramid of mystery. Subsequent illustrations are good examples of Millais' technique with group scenes. 'The Court' (plate 15) captures the hubbub and movement prior to the start of the courtroom proceedings. Millais seems to have made no effort to follow Trollope's jumbled description of the seating arrangements; Trollope himself noted in his bound set of proofs only that 'Lady Mason is the lady lifting her veil'. 'Lady Mason leaving the Court' (plate 16) is a kind of procession from the court, and one wherein the ubiquitous men's hats seem for once to lend solemnity. In both illustrations the black clothes of Lady Mason and her widow companion, together with the dark attire of some of the men, are impressive and strong without being heavy-handed. 'Bridget Bolster in Court' (plate 17) is another well-worked group scene in which we see little but the faces of lawyers and court officials on different levels as they look out at us, while Bridget Bolster is seen only from the back. The last two illustrations of Lady Mason are companion pieces: in the first, 'Farewell!' (plate 18), Lady Mason embraces Mrs Orme, and the two huge black spreading dresses blend, in what is again a successful though risky technique, the overall outline of the two figures being reminiscent of numerous renderings of the Visitation; in the second,

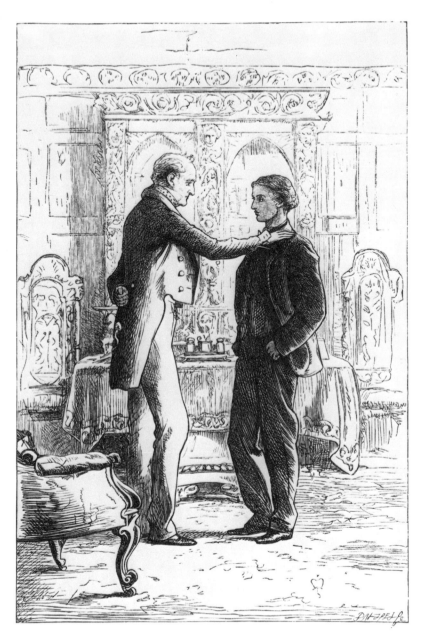

SIR PEREGRINE AND HIS HEIR.

20. J. E. Millais. *Orley Farm*

Over their Wine.

21. J. E. Millais. *Orley Farm*

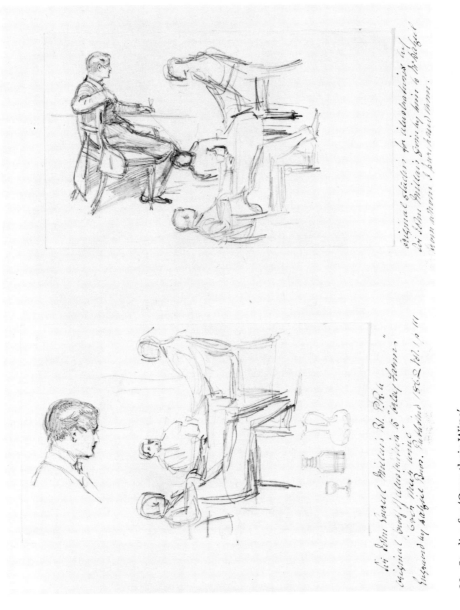

22. Studies for 'Over their Wine'

originally also called 'Farewell!' but altered in the third issue of the first edition to 'Sir Peregrine Orme's great love' (plate 19), Lady Mason and Orme embrace on parting, in a drawing poignant but not sentimental.

In Lady Mason's story, Trollope's 'nearest approach . . . to the depth and force of tragedy',[28] Millais has followed carefully, and the result is collaboration of the first order between artist and author. Indeed, at one point, Trollope, in describing Lady Mason on the evening before her trial, refers to a previous illustration:

> In an early part of this story I have endeavoured to describe how this woman sat alone, with deep sorrow in her heart and deep thought on her mind. . . . The idea, however, which the reader will have conceived of her as she sat there will have come to him from the skill of the artist, and not from the words of the writer. If that drawing is now near him, let him go back to it. Lady Mason was again sitting in the same room— that pleasant room, looking out through the verandah on to the sloping lawn, and in the same chair; one hand again rested open on the arm of the chair, while the other supported her face as she leaned upon her elbow. (Chapter lxiii)

Trollope, in suggesting that the reader look back at the early illustration, reveals that he himself had done so. In the earlier description we read simply that Lady Mason 'seated herself in her accustomed chair'; the details mentioned in the latter passage are in fact a description of Millais' drawing.

Sir Peregrine Orme, unbending in his honesty, honourable to a fault, opinionated yet lovable, has received from Millais' pencil a remarkable degree of individualisation. The old gentleman we first meet in 'Sir Peregrine and his Heir' (plate 20) is the same person we see later in 'Over their Wine' (plate 21), 'Why should I not' (plate 23), and whom we have seen twice pictured with Lady Mason. Lack of individualisation is what prompted Trollope's displeasure with 'Mr. Chaffanbrass and Mr. Solomon Aram' (plate 24) in which Millais depicted Lady Mason's barrister and her attorney. In Trollope's bound set of proofs he wrote. 'This alone, among the set, is not a good illustration. I know not which is Chaffanbrass, but neither can be like him.'[29] From the text, we know as well as Trollope that Chaffanbrass is the figure reclining on the sofa.

Of the less sombre illustrations accompanying the Noningsby episodes, 'The Drawing-Room at Noningsby' (plate 25) is representative.

" Why should I not."

23. J. E. Millais. *Orley Farm*

Mr. Chaffanbrass and Mr. Solomon Aram.

24. J. E. Millais. *Orley Farm*

The Drawing-Room at Noningsby.

25. J. E. Millais. *Orley Farm*

Trollope's text exhibits his typically light and unobtrusive humour. Felix Graham by this time has received permission from her parents to ask for Madeline's hand, but anxious as he is, he has not the privacy to do so on this occasion: 'There sat the judge, closely intent no doubt upon his book, but wide awake. There also sat Lady Staveley, fast asleep certainly; but with a wondrous power of hearing even in her sleep' (Chapter lxv). In Millais' drawing, Graham's frustration shows plainly. Another drawing from this group, 'Christmas at Noningsby—Evening' (plate 26) is the most lighthearted in the book; indeed, it is the most cheerful among all of Millais' illustrations for Trollope.

In addition to the central story of Lady Mason and the sub-plot of the young people, *Orley Farm* has the comic-relief episodes of the Moulder–Kantwise group, for which Millais has supplied two illustrations. The first, 'There is nothing like iron, Sir; nothing' (plate 27), is especially fine in its controlled humour. The scene is the Commercial Room of the Bull Inn, Leeds; Trollope's description of Moulder and Kantwise is almost Dickensian:

The first man who entered was short and very fat;—so fat that he could not have seen his own knees for some considerable time past. His face rolled with fat, as also did all his limbs. His eyes were large, and bloodshot. He wore no beard, and therefore showed plainly the triple bagging of his fat chin. In spite of his overwhelming fatness, there was something in his face that was masterful and almost vicious. His body had been overcome by eating, but not as yet his spirit,—one would be inclined to say. This was Mr. Moulder. . . .

The other was a little spare man in the hardware line, of the name of Kantwise. . . . He looked as though a skin rather too small for the purpose had been drawn over his head and face, so that his forehead and cheeks and chin were tight and shiny. His eyes were small and green, always moving about in his head, and were seldom used by Mr. Kantwise in the ordinary way. At whatever he looked he looked sideways. . . . His nose . . . seemed to have been compressed almost into nothing by that skin-squeezing operation. It was long enough, taking the measurement down the bridge, and projected sufficiently, counting the distance from the upper lip; but it had all the properties of a line; it possessed length without breadth. There was nothing in it from side to side. If you essayed to pull it, your fingers would meet. (Chapter vi)

Christmas at Noningsby.—Evening.

26. J. E. Millais. *Orley Farm*

Moulder and Kantwise are regular denizens of the Commercial Room; lawyer Dockwrath by rights ought not to be there at all. In Millais' drawing, Moulder, who had his doubts about Dockwrath's presence, is sleeping off his hearty dinner. Kantwise, ever eager for a sale, is demonstrating for the lawyer his metal furniture ('all gilt in real Louey catorse'). Having assembled his tables and chairs, Kantwise stepped nimbly up onto a round card table:

> In that position he skilfully brought his feet together, so that his weight was directly on the leg, and gracefully waved his hands over his head. James and Boots stood by admiring, with open mouths, and Mr. Dockwrath, with his hands in his pockets, was meditating whether he could not give the order without complying with the terms as to ready money.

Millais' drawing, with its scrupulous attention to detail, is precisely what we should expect from him at his best: Kantwise, for example, with his long thin nose, his ballet-like position, his head turned away from Dockwrath for whom all the display and salesmanship are intended, seems perfectly to accommodate the text. And yet Millais has carefully avoided descending to caricature, close as Trollope himself had approached it on this occasion.

Any discussion of the illustrations of *Orley Farm* must include the two outdoor scenes, the first of which, called simply 'Orley Farm' (plate 28), was used as frontispiece for the first volume of the book edition. Orley Farm itself was modelled on 'Julians Hill', the commodious though second and smaller Harrow residence of the Trollope family, and the home from which in 1834 they were forced because of debts to flee to the continent. ('Hamworth' and 'Hamworth Hill' of the novel are echoes of Harrow and Harrow-on-the-Hill.)

Millais probably found Trollope's written description, for all its apparent clarity, difficult to follow, for in a letter to Chapman Trollope spoke of the possibility of having the building photographed or of Millais' going out to see it.[30] A photograph (plate 29), remarkably like Millais' drawing, may have been the source for the illustration.[31] Trollope's text, written from memory of a place he had not seen in a quarter of a century, reads in part:

[Sir Joseph Mason] had gradually added to it and ornamented it till it

" There is nothing is nothing like iron, Sir ; nothing."

27. J. E. Millais. *Orley Farm*

ORLEY FARM.

28. J. E. Millais. *Orley Farm*

29. Photograph of the Harrow farmhouse, the original 'Orley Farm'

was commodious, irregular, picturesque, and straggling . . . it consisted of three buildings of various heights, attached to each other, and standing in a row. . . . [The lower building] was two stories high, but the rooms were low, and the roof steep and covered with tiles. The next portion . . . also was tiled, and the rooms were nearly as low; but there were three stories, and the building therefore was considerably higher . . . . [Later] he added on another step to the house at Orley Farm. On this occasion he built a good dining-room, with a drawing-room over it, and bed-room over that; and this portion of the edifice was slated.

The whole stood in one line fronting on to a large lawn which fell steeply away from the house into an orchard at the bottom. This lawn was cut in terraces, and here and there upon it there stood apple-trees of ancient growth; for here had been the garden of the old farm-house. They were large, straggling trees, such as do not delight the eyes of modern gardeners. . . . The face of the house from one end to the other was covered with vines and passion-flowers, for the aspect was due south; and as the whole of the later addition was faced by a verandah, which also, as regarded the ground-floor, ran along the middle building, the place in summer was pretty enough. As I have said before, it was irregular and straggling, but at the same time roomy and picturesque. Such was Orley Farm-house. (Chapter i)

Of this passage Bradford Booth remarked that writing could scarcely be less precious.[32] Millais, on the other hand, has chosen to idyllicise the scene, not quite in the fashion of G. J. Pinwell, or J. W. North, but in a manner somewhat removed from the realism of most of his drawings for Trollope. Here, for example, Millais has added ('on his own hook', Rossetti would have said) a milkmaid and cow, meant no doubt to contribute a bucolic touch—although one would not ordinarily expect to see cows milked in an orchard, and from the wrong side at that. The house itself seems remote and quiet, but one has it constantly in the mind's eye as one reads the story of Lady Mason: this was the attractive house and grounds she so desired for her son, and for which she had forged a will and perjured herself, the house which after twenty years' possession she and her son will surrender at the novel's end.

Finally, one comes to 'Monkton Grange' (plate 30), the assemblage before the hunt: 'a special hunting morning—special, because the meet was in some degree a show meet, appropriate for ladies, at a comfortable distance from Noningsby, and affording a chance of amusement to those

" Monkton Grange."

30. J. E. Millais. *Orley Farm*

who sat in carriages as well as to those on horseback. . . . Monkton Grange is an old farm-house . . . but it still possesses the marks of ancient respectability and even of grandeur' (Chapter xxviii). Millais, using branches of huge trees to frame the upper half of his drawing, has brought together ladies, gentlemen, horses, dogs, and carriages against a background of the gabled house. It is another of the relatively few crowded scenes Millais drew for Trollope, and enough to make one wish he had attempted more illustrations of this sort. The drawing, which evokes so well the elegant Victorian country life of which Trollope is the acknowledged chronicler, is perhaps the best known illustration in the Trollope canon. The fox hunt seems the perfect symbol for the leisured world of rural England, and as hunting was Trollope's second greatest passion (writing was surely first), he must have been especially thankful for Millais' sensitive rendering.

The Small House at Allington

Trollope's next illustrated novel, again in collaboration with Millais, was *The Small House at Allington*, which appeared in the *Cornhill* from September 1862 to April 1864 and was published in two volumes in March 1864. The book edition contained all eighteen full-page illustrations but none of the nineteen very fine chapter-heading vignettes. (Two representative vignettes are reproduced in plates 31 and 32.) Evidently, Trollope chose the subjects for illustration; in November 1862 he wrote to Smith:

> As regards the last three numbers Mrs Millais wrote to 'your' Mr Williams [Smith's assistant] for the subjects—& I sent them thro Mr Williams. . . . Guided by this I have supposed he has wished to have his subjects closely marked out. I will go on doing so—& w^d suggest that you s^d always send the paper to him. If he chooses to change the subject I shall not complain. I feel however that the author can select the subjects better than the artist—having all the feeling of the story at his fingers end.[33]

The Small House at Allington makes a number of special claims for attention. It is of course the penultimate novel of the Barsetshire series (although Trollope capriciously had not at first wished to include it in the collected edition of the Barsetshire novels, 1878); in Johnny Eames it provides us with a partial self-portrait of Trollope as hobbledehoy and youthful civil servant; it acts as a preface to the entire Palliser series and serves as a link between the two series.

The main story concerns Lily Dale, Adolphus Crosbie and Eames; after Crosbie jilts Lily for the position he hopes a marriage with a daughter of an Earl will bring him, Lily is unable to give herself to Eames, who has loved her throughout. Millais, in his eighteen illustrations, drew Eames six times, Lily and Crosbie four each, and Crosbie's wife Alexandrina de Courcy twice. Millais is least successful with Lily; like other illustrators of the period he had difficulty in individualising beautiful young women. Perhaps the best representation of her comes in 'And have I not really loved you?' (plate 33), where she is seen in the garden at Allington with Eames. He, having learned of Lily's engagement to Crosbie, has sought her out and impetuously told her that he nonetheless loves her. (He will continue in his frustrated love for her throughout this novel and *The Last Chronicle of Barset*.) In Millais' drawing, Lily has her eyes modestly cast down; she knows that as an engaged woman it is improper to hear such protestations, but she is unwilling to be harsh with her childhood friend. As their eyes do not meet, neither do their figures touch. It is an attractive drawing, except for the somewhat awkward position of Lily's right arm.

Eames is fairly well drawn again in the final illustration of the book. He stands discouraged on the little bridge over the brook that divides the Allington and De Guest properties and tells Lady Julia De Guest the news of Lily's final denial, 'She has refused me and it is all over' (plate 35). Millais as usual has been careful not to sentimentalise his subject, avoiding even the suggestion of an agonised face. The downward position of Eames' head is sufficient.

Millais is even more successful with the villain—although that word is too strong for the weak but not altogether conscienceless Crosbie. In 'That might do' (plate 36), Crosbie is already beginning to receive punishment for his perfidy to Lily. Part of the preliminaries for his marriage involve setting up house and shopping for furniture. Trollope describes some of the activity:

It was pleasant to see the Ladies Amelia [Crosbie's future sister-in-law] and Alexandrina [his future wife], as they sat within a vast emporium of carpets in Bond Street, asking questions of the four men who were waiting upon them, putting their heads together and whispering,

The Small House at Allington.

CHAPTER VII.

THE BEGINNING OF TROUBLES.

ILY, as she parted with her lover in the garden, had required of him to attend upon her the next morning as he went to his shooting, and in obedience to this command he appeared on Mrs. Dale's lawn after breakfast, accompanied by Bernard and two dogs. The men had guns in their hands, and were got up with all proper sporting appurtenances, but it so turned out that they did not reach the stubble-fields on the farther side of the road until after luncheon. And may it not be fairly doubted whether croquet is not as good as shooting when a man is in love?

It will be said that Bernard Dale was not in love; but they who bring such accusation against him, will bring it falsely. He was in love with his cousin Bell according to his manner and fashion. It was not his nature to love Bell as John Eames loved Lily; but then neither would his nature bring him into such a trouble as that which the charms of Amelia Roper had brought upon the poor clerk from the Income-tax Office. Johnny was susceptible, as the word goes; whereas Captain Dale was a man who had his feelings well under control. He was not one to make a fool of himself about a girl, or to die of a broken heart; but, nevertheless, he would probably love his wife when he got a wife, and would be a careful father to his children.

They were very intimate with each other now,—these four. It was Bernard and Adolphus, or sometimes Apollo, and Bell and Lily among them; and Crosbie found it to be pleasant enough. A new position of

31. J. E. Millais. Vignette, *The Small House at Allington*

The Small House at Allington.

CHAPTER XVI.

Mr. Crosbie meets an old Clergyman on his way to Courcy Castle.

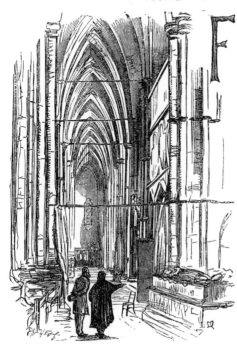

FOR the first mile or two of their journey Crosbie and Bernard Dale sat, for the most part, silent in their gig. Lily, as she ran down to the churchyard corner and stood there looking after them with her loving eyes, had not been seen by them. But the spirit of her devotion was still strong upon them both, and they felt that it would not be well to strike at once into any ordinary topic of conversation. And, moreover, we may presume that Crosbie did feel much at thus parting from such a girl as Lily Dale, with whom he had lived in close intercourse for the last six weeks, and whom he loved with all his heart,—with all the heart that he had for such purposes. In those doubts as to his marriage which had troubled him he had never expressed to himself any disapproval of Lily. He had not taught himself to think that she was other than he would have her be, that he might thus give himself an excuse for parting from her. Not as yet, at any rate, had he had recourse to that practice, so common with men who wish to free themselves from the bonds with which they have permitted themselves to be bound. Lily had been too sweet to his eyes, to his touch, to all his senses for that. He had enjoyed too keenly the pleasure of being with her, and of hearing her tell him that she loved him, to allow of his being personally tired of her. He had not been so spoilt by his club life but that he had taken exquisite pleasure in all her nice country ways, and soft, kind-hearted, womanly humour. He was

32. J. E. Millais. Vignette, *The Small House at Allington*

"AND HAVE I NOT REALLY LOVED YOU?"

33. J. E. Millais. *The Small House at Allington*

34. Photograph of original pencil drawing on wood block for 'And have I not really loved you?'

"SHE HAS REFUSED ME AND IT IS ALL OVER."

35. J. E. Millais. *The Small House at Allington*

"THAT MIGHT DO."

36. J. E. Millais. *The Small House at Allington*

calculating accurately as to extra twopences a yard, and occasioning as much trouble as it was possible for them to give. It was pleasant because they managed their large hoops cleverly among the huge rolls of carpets, because they were enjoying themselves thoroughly, and taking to themselves the homage of the men as clearly their due. But it was not pleasant to look at Crosbie, who was fidgeting to get away to his office, to whom no power of choosing in the matter was really given, and whom the men regarded as being altogether supernumerary. . . . Crosbie felt for the men who were hauling about the huge heaps of material; but Lady Amelia sat as composed as though it were her duty to inspect every yard of stuff in the warehouse. . . . 'That might do,' said Alexandrina. . . . And as she spoke she held her head gracefully on one side, and looked down upon the carpet doubtingly. Lady Amelia poked it with her parasol as though to test its durability, and whispered something about yellows showing the dirt. Crosbie took out his watch and groaned. (Chapter xl)

Millais gives meticulous attention to Trollope's description—the ladies comfortably seated, their leisurely attitude, the tilt of Alexandrina's head, the probing of Amelia's parasol; four attendants are seen, one of whom (Millais' own touch) is holding his spectacles as long suffering but tired people are sometimes wont to do. Crosbie's restrained impatience is evident. But the engraving is more than the pictorialisation of a humorous moment. The scene is symbolic of much of what has gone before and what will come afterwards in Crosbie's courtship, engagement, and marriage: the haughty attitude of the noble De Courcys, the penny-pinching they engage in, the interference of Crosbie's in-laws in his affairs, Crosbie's belated desire to get out of the marriage altogether. Trollope's humour has been illustrated here, but the case of Adolphus Crosbie and Alexandrina De Courcy is sad as well. The unhappy side of Crosbie's marriage is spelled out plainly in the illustration that came to be used as the frontispiece for volume two of the book edition. Both Crosbie and Alexandrina find their marriage cold and dull; they are irritable and quarrelsome with each other: 'Why, on earth, on Sunday?' (plate 37) shows Crosbie's reaction to the news that they are to visit her sister and brother-in-law. The facial features of both Crosbie and Alexandrina are carefully delineated; they are identifiable persons realistically drawn. Alexandrina, for example, is somewhat heavy and clearly no beauty; her looks do not belie her years. Even their postures reveal discontent.

Even more discontented with family life, and a much older campaigner

64

"WHY, ON EARTH, ON SUNDAY?"

37. J. E. Millais. *The Small House at Allington*

'DEVOTEDLY ATTACHED TO THE YOUNG MAN!'

38. J. E. Millais. *The Small House at Allington*

"LET ME BEG YOU TO THINK OVER THE MATTER AGAIN."

39. J. E. Millais. *The Small House at Allington*

THE BOARD

40. J. E. Millais. *The Small House at Allington*

in the field, is the Earl De Courcy, Alexandrina's father. Millais' drawing shows him denouncing to his wife their daughter's impending engagement to Crosbie. 'Devotedly attached to the young man!' (plate 38) is his sarcastic rejoinder to the Countess' explanation of the match. Yet he is correct—Crosbie is after an aristocratic connection, and Alexandrina simply wants to get away from home at any cost. Millais was especially adept at drawing old men, as adept as Trollope was at creating them. Millais' Squire Dale is another such instance, particularly in the illustration that shows him capping his arguments to Mrs Dale against her leaving the Small House with the words 'Let me beg you to think over the matter again' (plate 39). Mrs Dale is a stock figure, her hand raised as if to ward off both trouble and Dale's words. But the squire is individualised. Other old men are excellently (and humorously) drawn in 'The Board' (plate 40). The commissioners pictured here include Sir Raffle Buffle, Trollope's fussy bullying bureaucrat, seen with his back to the fire; Mr Butterwell to the left; at the right Mr Optimist, scarcely five feet tall, 'standing behind the arm chair, rubbing his hands together, and longing for the departure of Sir Raffle, in order that he might sit down'—Optimist is also succeeding to Buffle's chairmanship. Seated, and indifferent to such amenities, is Major Fiasco, 'a discontented, broken-hearted, silent man, who had been sent to the General Committee Office some few years before because he was not wanted anywhere else' (Chapter xxviii).

But it is on another old man, Mr Harding, whose story in *The Warden* had been the seed for the entire Barsetshire series, that Millais lavishes his most careful attention—although he seems to have erred in reversing his subject. The illustration bore the legend 'There is Mr. Harding coming out of the Deanery' in the *Cornhill* but ' "He is of that sort that they make the angels of," said the Verger' in the book issue (plate 41). On first reading, the episode called 'Mr. Crosbie Meets an Old Clergyman on his Way to Courcy Castle' (Chapter xvi) may seem unnecessary, or, worse, an excuse to expose the reader to a little précis of *The Warden, Barchester Towers*, and parts of *Framley Parsonage*. However, a more careful reading, such as that suggested by A. O. J. Cockshut, can be revealing. For one thing, Harding is the 'moral touchstone' wherever he appears in the Barset novels. Here Crosbie is on his way to Courcy Castle where, as Trollope has hinted, he will betray his betrothed for Lady Alexandrina. But as Cockshut points out, Trollope uses his moral touchstone with great care: we find no 'impassioned plea for fidelity from the old man to the young, or . . . touching story of days long ago which will mysteriously fit the present situation'. Rather we hear only

"There is Mr. Harding coming out of the Deanery."

41. J. E. Millais. *The Small House at Allington*

MR. PALLISER AND LADY DUMBELLO.

42. J. E. Millais. *The Small House at Allington*

rambling talk on Harding's part as 'the innocence of old age is confronted with the corruption of youth'.[34] In the illustration, the verger is pointing out Harding to Crosbie prior to their meeting a few moments later. Trollope describes Harding:

> He was a little, withered, shambling old man, with bent shoulders, dressed in knee-breeches and long black gaiters, which hung rather loosely about his poor old legs,—rubbing his hands one over the other as he went. And yet he walked quickly; not tottering as he walked, but with an uncertain, doubtful step. . . . Crosbie felt that he had never seen a face on which traits of human kindness were more plainly written.

All this is literally and touchingly present in Millais' drawing, but so are the subtle contrasts of age to youth, spirituality to worldliness, and idealism to cynicism.

As has been noted, *The Small House at Allington* provides a sort of preface to the six novels today called the Palliser novels, since in this book the character from whom the series derives its name makes his first appearance. Here the young Plantagenet Palliser, far more rash than one who knew him only from the later novels would have expected, is contemplating running off with Lord Dumbello's wife. To these episodes Millais devotes only one illustration, 'Mr. Palliser and Lady Dumbello' (plate 42), but it was used as frontispiece for the first volume of the book edition. It is difficult to say whether Trollope, when he wrote *The Small House at Allington*, had in mind making Palliser the keystone of a long series of novels—most probably he did not. In any event Palliser became his single most elaborated character, and one is surely safe in presuming that Trollope included this drawing among those by Millais of which he wrote in the *Autobiography*: 'I have carried on some of those characters from book to book, and have had my own early ideas impressed indelibly on my memory by the excellence of his delineations.'[35] In the *Small House at Allington*, Millais had little physical description of Palliser to follow, other than that 'he was about five-and-twenty years of age. . . . He dressed very quietly, never changing the colour or form of his garments; and in society was quiet, reserved, and very often silent. He was tall, slight, and not ill-looking; but more than this cannot be said for his personal appearance—except, indeed, this, that no one could mistake him for other than a gentleman' (Chapter xxiii). In the scene illustrated,

Palliser passes a moment's harmless conversation with Lady Dumbello, who is 'sitting, alone, in a large, low chair, made without arms, so as to admit the full expansion of her dress, but hollowed and round at the back, so as to afford her the support that was necessary to her'. We have heard countless times in *Framley Parsonage* and the present novel of the peerless if cold beauty of Lady Dumbello, and Millais had in fact included her in the upper left portion of the crowded 'Lady Lufton and the Duke of Omnium' illustration for the earlier novel. Here he gives her a classical profile and at the same time invests her with a look altogether in keeping with her reputation for constant and peculiar taciturnity; she is not shy, she simply never says much. Palliser, intelligent, bookish, earnest, is shy enough. The heads of two gossips, one turned to look, are placed between Palliser and Lady Dumbello; he is tall and stands above such rumour-mongers; she is completely indifferent to them. The involvement will of course come to nothing, in spite of Plantagenet's later foolish resolve to risk all, including the wrath of his uncle, the Duke of Omnium, whose presumptive heir Palliser is. Lady Dumbello, at one word from her mother, will send Palliser scurrying into the arms of Lady Glencora. But, unfortunately, it fell to other artists to illustrate the Pallisers' early married life in *Can You Forgive Her?*

Phineas Finn: The Irish Member

The consecutive collaboration of Millais and Trollope was to have continued for at least one more novel. Upon completing the writing of *The Small House* early in 1863 Trollope began a novel, *Rachel Ray*, for the evangelical monthly *Good Words*. (It was in this publication and in this same year that Millais was publishing his now famous drawings of the Parables.) But the editor, Norman Macleod, faced with criticism from a rival evangelical journal for announcing a story by 'this year's chief sensation writer', and aware of *Rachel Ray*'s distinctly worldly bias, rejected the novel. Trollope wrote to Millais:

> [*Good Words*] has thrown me over. They write me word that I am too wicked. I tell you at once because of the projected, and now not-to-be-accomplished-drawings. They have tried to serve God and the devil together, and finding that goodness pays best, have thrown over me and the devil. I won't try to set you against them because you can do

43. J. E. Millais. Watercolour version, frontispiece for *Rachel Ray*,
Seventh Edition

Parables and other fish fit for their net; but I am altogether unsuited to the regenerated![36]

Trollope arranged to have Chapman & Hall bring out *Rachel Ray* in two volumes, and the only vestige of the originally projected illustrations was a frontispiece for the one-volume 'Seventh Edition' of 1864—an exceedingly rare book today. Reproduced here is Millais' later watercolour version of that illustration (plate 43).

There followed three novels illustrated by others, *Can You Forgive Her?*, *The Claverings*, and *The Last Chronicle of Barset*. But in 1867, when Trollope was embarking upon his editorship of *St Paul's Magazine*, he was doubtless able to plead special circumstances and succeeded in bringing Millais back for one more novel. He also asked Millais to do a vignette of St Paul's Cathedral for the magazine cover, and the drawing, though unsigned, may well be his. In any event, Millais, who had by this time altogether given up black-and-white work, illustrated *Phineas Finn*, and the words 'With Illustrations by J. E. Millais' appeared very prominently on the magazine wrapper, although he did no work for *St Paul's* other than the drawings for Trollope's novel. *Phineas Finn* appeared from October 1867 to May 1869 with one illustration for each monthly instalment; all twenty plates were included in the two-volume book edition published in March 1869.

Millais' illustrations for *Phineas Finn* are slightly below the standard he set for himself in the earlier novels. His painting had become less minutely elaborated, and the illustrations too have become freer and less detailed. By itself such a change need not have been for the worse, but Millais seems to have taken less care with these drawings. Certainly the failure to individualise characters, especially young women, became more pronounced. Moreover, the illustrations are less varied. Most of the *Phineas Finn* drawings feature two characters; there are no group scenes or architectural drawings.

It is not known whether Trollope continued his earlier practice of selecting the subject while allowing the artist the final word. The choice is particularly telling in this novel. For one thing, *Phineas Finn*, the first of his 'semi-political novels' ('As I was debarred from expressing my opinions in the House of Commons,' he wrote, 'I took this method of declaring myself'), contains no illustrations of the political scenes. Trollope explained that he believed his readers would not be interested in the political aspects of the novel: 'If I wrote politics for my own sake, I

"You don't quite know Mr. Kennedy yet."

44. J. E. Millais. *Phineas Finn*

must put in love and intrigue, social incidents, with perhaps a dash of sport, for the sake of my readers.'[37] What he did was to crowd the novel with love affairs and a number of fascinating women: Lady Laura Standish, Lady Glencora, Violet Effingham, Madame Max Goesler. Very unlike these memorable, witty, ambitious women is Mary Flood Jones, the simple Irish girl whom Finn eventually marries. In this connection one can note with Gordon Ray that Trollope had Mary Flood Jones illustrated five times, including both frontispieces of the book edition, as if to make up for the neglect of her in the text.[38]

After Finn himself, who is centre stage most of the time and who appears in half of the illustrations, Lady Laura, who, as Trollope said, is the best character in the book, received most of Millais' attention, eight plates in all. Laura, whose family is politically prominent, adopts Phineas, newly elected to Parliament, as her protégé and 'political pupil'; she is instrumental in getting him a government post, and in securing for him her father's pocket borough after Finn loses his Irish seat. She is, in fact, in love with him. Trollope describes her as 'about five feet seven in height . . . she carried her height well. There was something of nobility in her gait, and she seemed thus to be taller than her inches. Her hair was in truth red. . . . Her face was very fair, though it lacked that softness which we all love in women. Her eyes, which were large and bright, and very clear, never seemed to quail. . . . Her nose was perfectly cut, but was rather large, having the slightest possible tendency to be aquiline' (Chapter iv). She is first illustrated in Chapter vi, a drawing-room scene in which she tells Phineas not to dismiss the wealthy Robert Kennedy too lightly: 'You don't quite know Mr. Kennedy yet' (plate 44). She is well drawn, her face answering nicely to Trollope's words, the hands (sometimes carelessly rendered by illustrators) perfect, her dress sumptuous. Phineas is indeed the handsome young man so many women will find irresistible. The moment depicted seems relaxed and insignificant. But the next illustration shows Laura and Phineas in a state anything but calm and reveals the import of her earlier words. For within a few months, in spite of her love for Phineas, she accepts an offer of marriage from Kennedy, largely with a view to settling her brother's debts. In a scene of intense emotion at Kennedy's estate in Scotland, Finn has sought out Laura to ask for her hand, only to have her tell him that she had yesterday accepted Kennedy; to Finn she can only say, 'I wish to regard you as a dear friend, —both of my own and of my husband' (plate 45). Phineas, dressed in Scottish garb, hands thrust into his pockets, angry with her and with

"I wish to regard you as a dear friend,—both of my own and of my husband."

45. J. E. Millais. *Phineas Finn*

"I will send for Dr. Macnuthrie at once."

46. J. E. Millais. *Phineas Finn*

himself, holds back as she extends her hand. As events throughout *Phineas Finn* and *Phineas Redux* prove, the brother–sister relationship she proposed is one which Laura, with her deep feelings for Phineas, will find impossible. He, on the other hand, will quickly recover his affections, fall in love with Violet Effingham, nearly accept Madame Max Goesler, marry Mary Flood Jones, and after his wife's death, eventually marry Madame Max.

Laura's unhappy marriage is realised by Millais in an illustration for the chapter called 'Lady Laura's Headache'. Kennedy has proved morbidly religious and despotic, and Laura finds life with him unbearable to the point of illness. But her love for the now departed Phineas is a contributing factor also. In the scene illustrated, Laura has as much as told Kennedy that it is life with him that brings on her headaches. His reply is 'I will send for Dr. Macnuthrie at once' (plate 46). Such impersonal action is the only remedy he can think of, but, while the reader's sympathy is with Laura, she must share the blame for their unhappy state. This plate, like one other in *Phineas Finn*, represents a departure from Millais' usual practice in that it is wider than it is high and could not be printed upright on the page. This sideways positioning looks unattractive and can distract the reader. Perhaps more significant, however, is Millais' departure from his usual elaborated background. Here the rich detail, a carry-over from Pre-Raphaelite days, and seen so often in his earlier illustrations for Trollope, has given way to rather ugly and ungainly cross-hatching. Yet the figures are impressive, and Kennedy's unctuous movement toward the door is very real.

Further deterioration in the Kennedy marriage is epitomised in the drawing called 'So she burned the morsel of paper' (plate 47). By this time Laura's devotion to Phineas and Kennedy's extravagant though not unfounded jealousy have come out into the open. Kennedy desired her to have no communication with Phineas, and when she denied that there had been any of late, Kennedy pointed to the telegram in her hand and quickly left the room. But although the telegram, announcing Finn's election, had come in fact from her cousin, she would not stoop to defend herself, and she burned the evidence. Millais' drawing shows her, telegram in hand, looking into the fire; her face in half shadow is still recognisable as that of the woman seen in previous illustrations, but her expression and posture betray sadness and defeat.

In the final illustration of Lady Laura, she, determined to leave her husband because he has accused her of being Phineas' lover, insists that

" So she burned the morsel of paper."

47. J. E. Millais. *Phineas Finn*

Phineas had no alternative but to read the letter.

48. J. E. Millais. *Phineas Finn*

" Oh, Phineas ; surely a thousand a-year will be very nice."

49. J. E. Millais. *Phineas Finn*

Phineas read her letter informing Kennedy of her return to her father's house. The title, again directly from the text, is significant: 'Phineas had no alternative but to read the letter' (plate 48); his affections are far from her, and only from a sense of duty does he hear out the news of these unfortunate developments. Phineas appears somewhat stiff and plainly anxious to pull away from her. Laura, drawn with high eyebrows and a strong nose, looks almost Mediterranean, but her features are again consistent with those in earlier drawings of her. But the three years that have passed show in her haggard face. Finn too is older and slightly heavier; he clearly has advanced in bearing and self-possession. Laura's sad story, in this book at least, has finished, and the illustrations have accompanied her at strategic points and contributed much to the way we see her.

Finn's own fortunes do not prosper. Unsuccessful in his romantic pursuit of first Laura, then Violet Effingham, he is too proud to accept Madame Max's bold proposal. He resigns his seat in Parliament rather than vote with his party against Irish tenant rights. Returned to Ireland, he becomes engaged to Mary Flood Jones, his prospects somewhat bolstered by a last-minute appointment as Poor Law inspector at £1000 per annum. It is a contrived and therefore unsatisfactory ending, but Millais' illustration strikes the necessary note of domestic tranquillity. 'Oh, Phineas; surely a thousand a-year will be very nice' (plate 49) has Mary and Phineas looking at the letter announcing the appointment. The two figures blend together in relaxed fashion; none of the stress and tension connected with the Laura–Phineas drawings is present.

With less important characters in this novel Millais has been less successful. Lord Chiltern, so wrathful as to be dangerous, was probably too violent a subject for Millais' taste. Certainly the drawing of Chiltern and Finn quarrelling, 'I do not choose that there should be a riot here' (Chapter xxxvii), is among the worst Millais ever did. On the other hand, the two illustrations featuring the old Duke of Omnium are effective. The second, 'And I ain't in a hurry either,—am I, Mamma?' (plate 50) takes for its subject the kind of subtle but dramatic domestic moment Trollope loved to develop: Lady Glencora and her child had been shown into the drawing-room at the very moment in which the old Duke might have proposed marriage to Madame Max Goesler. Were such a marriage to take place, Glencora's child might lose his expectations—for he is in line for the dukedom. Madame Max manages the situation gracefully, and conversation turns to the boy's father, so busy working

" And I ain't in a hurry either,--am I, Mamma ? "

50. J. E. Millais. *Phineas Finn*

for his country and, as the old man remarks, in no hurry to become duke. Whereupon the child says that he is in no hurry either. Millais' drawing catches all of the tension. Moreover, the Duke, balding and heavier now, some ten years older than on that occasion of his brief encounter with Lady Lufton in *Framley Parsonage*, is superbly drawn, as is the child. Lady Glencora is also good, if somewhat matronly, in the only drawing Millais ever did of the character whom, together with Plantagenet Palliser, Trollope rightly regarded as his supreme achievement. The artist has grouped to one side the Duke, the child, and Lady Glencora, the family as it were, with Madame Max the outsider standing apart to the right. The only weakness of the illustration is Madame Max, whose face is characterless and very poorly drawn.

Phineas Finn, for all its excellence, ends somewhat abruptly and artificially. It was, as Trollope said, but half of what he considered one novel. The other half, *Phineas Redux*, did not appear until 1873, and by that time Millais had long given up illustration. His only further work for Trollope was a single illustration (plate 51), which became the frontispiece for *Kept in the Dark*, published in 1882, the year of Trollope's death.

Millais' illustrations for Trollope succeed for a variety of reasons: Millais' superb draughtsmanship, his willingness to work with the medium,[39] his exacting care with illustration. On this last point the remarks of Millais' son are doubtless valid, in spite of some filial overstatement: 'Very few people have any idea of the labour and care that he expended on these drawings. Each one of them was to him a carefully thought-out picture, worthy of the best work that he could put into it. . . . The money he received for these drawings was but a nominal recompense for the labour bestowed upon them; for, unless perfectly satisfied with the finished production, he would tear it up at once, even if he had spent whole days upon it, scamped work in any shape being an abomination in his eyes.'[40]

Even more important, and here we have Trollope's own word, was Millais' willingness to *illustrate* the text, to follow another's ideas:

Altogether [Millais] drew from my tales eighty-seven[41] drawings, and I do not think that more conscientious work was ever done by man. Writers of novels know well—and so ought readers of novels to have learned—that there are two modes of illustrating, either of which may be adopted equally by a bad and by a good artist. To which class Mr. Millais belongs I need not say; but, as a good artist, it was open to him

'When the letter was completed, she found it to be one which she could not send.'

51. J. E. Millais. *Kept in the Dark*

simply to make a pretty picture, or to study the work of the author from whose writing he was bound to take his subject. I have too often found that the former alternative has been thought to be the better, as it certainly is the easier method. An artist will frequently dislike to subordinate his ideas to those of an author, and will sometimes be too idle to find out what those ideas are. But this artist was neither proud nor idle. In every figure he drew it was his object to promote the views of the writer whose work he had undertaken to illustrate, and he never spared himself any pains in studying that work, so as to enable himself to do so.[42]

Finally, the successful collaboration of Millais and Trollope resulted largely from a certain compatibility of artistic temper and similarity of approach. For in spite of all the misleading things that have been written about Trollope's 'photographic realism', his mode was indeed that of undistorted, richly-detailed, straightforward realism. That he recounted at length, even with perfectly uncanny accuracy, seemingly unimportant episodes in the lives of his characters—say, a lengthy conversation of only the slightest apparent connection with the story—has annoyed critics of his age and ours. But such was his method. Similarly Millais has been accused of the same seemingly indiscriminate attention to detail, the extreme care with which each leaf or reed was painted in the *Ophelia*, or, to come to an illustration for Trollope, the detailed crinoline dress that was said to have been more important than Lucy Robarts herself. A contemporary reviewer of *Framley Parsonage* put the matter succinctly and provocatively: 'Mr. Millais illustrates this fiction; and to the school of art represented by Mr. Millais among artists, belongs Mr. Trollope among the writers of fiction. He is a Pre-Raphaelite.'[43] The extent to which this assertion is literally true is unimportant. It is close enough. The Millais illustrations succeed; they are remarkably 'Trollopian'.

HABLOT KNIGHT BROWNE AND
E. TAYLOR

Can You Forgive Her?

After *Rachel Ray* came to be published without previous serialisation and therefore without illustrations, the collaboration between Millais and Trollope was not resumed in the next novel, *Can You Forgive Her?* The reason lay partly in Millais' unwillingness to take time away from his lucrative painting, and partly in the publisher's desire for economy. As early as the Moxon *Tennyson* Millais received £25 per drawing. By contrast, Miss Taylor, who was to do the latter half of *Can You Forgive Her?*, would receive five guineas. In any case, when the first shilling part of *Can You Forgive Her?* appeared in January 1864 the illustrations were by Hablot Knight Browne (1815–82). 'Phiz', as Browne was better known, had begun his long collaboration with Dickens in 1836 when he became the illustrator of *Pickwick* after the suicide of Robert Seymour. Browne played a considerable role in fixing in the reading public's mind many of Dickens' celebrated characters. Particularly adept at comic characters, Phiz was essentially a caricaturist and a fine one (much as some may prefer his more 'serious' work, especially the later 'dark plates'). For a time it was the fashion for critics to belittle his work as inferior to Cruikshank's, but one can argue that Browne was as effective an illustrator as the older artist, at least as far as collaboration with Dickens was concerned. In recent studies, John Harvey, while still holding Cruikshank superior, has much praise for Browne, and Q. D. Leavis believes that Browne was the better illustrator for Dickens.[1] Whatever one's opinion, Browne in fact illustrated ten of Dickens' novels, whereas Cruikshank did only *Oliver Twist* and *Sketches by Boz*.

In working with Browne, Dickens closely supervised the entire operation: he selected the subject for illustration, gave specific directions, examined a preliminary drawing, and made further suggestions and corrections before the final etching was made. Harvey thinks *Dombey* the high point of the collaboration; others see Browne's early caricatures as equally good.

But most would agree that there was a falling off after *Bleak House*, and that Browne's illustrations for *A Tale of Two Cities*—his last work for Dickens—were his least successful. Exactly when and why Dickens decided to drop Browne for Marcus Stone in *Our Mutual Friend* is difficult to ascertain. That Browne was dismayed is evident from a letter he wrote to Robert Young:

> Marcus [Stone] is no doubt to do Dickens. *I* have been a 'good boy', I believe. The plates in hand are all in good time, so that I do not know what's 'up', any more than you. Dickens probably thinks a new hand would give his old puppets a fresh look, or perhaps he does not like my illustrating Trollope neck-and-neck with him—though, by Jingo, he need fear no rivalry *there!* Confound all authors and publishers, say I. There is no pleasing one or t'other. I wish I had never had anything to do with the lot.[2]

But Browne had earlier had a falling out with Dickens; furthermore, after the death of Stone's father in 1859—he had been a companion of Dickens in his barnstorming theatre days—Dickens had been on the lookout to assist the young artist. Stone had been engaged in 1862 to illustrate the one-volume Library Editions of *Great Expectations*, *American Notes*, and *A Child's History of England*. Doubtless Harvey is correct in saying that neither the assumption that Dickens capriciously dismissed Browne nor the belief that Dickens grew with the times and came to prefer the new Sixties style of illustration is wholly satisfactory.[3]

But whatever the reasons for Dickens' dismissal of Browne, one can see from Browne's letter that all was not going well between himself and Trollope either. It should be remembered that Browne had worked for Dickens for more than two decades (the very name 'Phiz' had been taken to answer to 'Boz'), and Trollope, now very much a name himself, was probably displeased with being connected with another novelist's illustrator. Whether by design or not, none of Phiz's plates for Trollope was signed in any fashion, and he was called 'H. K. Browne' on the front cover of the shilling wrappers; the title page of the first book edition read simply 'With Illustrations'. Then too, Trollope undoubtedly realised that he was getting Browne's services at the fag end of his career and after his talent was largely exhausted. But Trollope's principal objection must have rested upon a recognition of the incompatibility of his own style with Browne's. Indeed, Trollope and Browne were as ill-attuned to each other as Dickens and Browne had been suited to each other. To say this is to underscore the very different approaches that Dickens and Trollope brought to fiction. For direct confirmation of the difference we need look no further than Trollope's estimation of Dickens:

> I do acknowledge that Mrs. Gamp, Micawber, Pecksniff, and others have become household words in every house, as though they were human beings; but to my judgement they are not human beings, nor are any of the characters human which Dickens has portrayed. It has been the peculiarity and the marvel of this man's power, that he has invested his puppets with a charm that has enabled him to dispense with human nature. . . . Nor is the pathos of Dickens human. It is stagey and melodramatic.[4]

Thus Trollope ranked Dickens below Thackeray and George Eliot among novelists of his day. In a word, Dickens' fiction was not 'realistic' enough. Trollope preferred simple predictable plots, not the involved dramatic turnings of Dickens; melodrama and extreme sentimentality were anathema to Trollope; burlesque and broad humour were not generally his métier. Trollope's low-keyed novels of domestic manners, which could be so ably illustrated by Millais, were surely not suitable for the artist who had unforgettably captured precisely those aspects of Dickens' work which Trollope in his own writing eschewed. (Even Browne's medium, etching, seems somehow incongruous in a Trollope novel.)

When one first looks at the illustrations for *Can You Forgive Her?* it seems as if Dickens' characters (of a diluted form—for the life had gone out of Browne's work) had strayed into the pages of Trollope. Browne attempted to make adjustments: here his characters are less severely caricatured, they are none of them deliberately disproportioned, and they assume no outrageous postures. Nevertheless they appear out of place in Trollope. It is not so much that Lady Midlothian in the illustration 'Would you mind shutting the window?' (Chapter ii) looks like Mrs. Pipchin— which she does—but that every character has the 'Dickens look', or, perhaps, the 'Phiz look', for the two are pretty much the same in the reader's mind. This Dickensian quality is especially unfortunate in the scenes from the two main plots, the love triangle of Alice Vavasor, George Vavasor and John Grey, and that of Lady Glencora, Plantagenet Palliser and Burgo Fitzgerald. The illustration titled 'Burgo Fitzgerald' (plate 52) will serve as an example. Trollope describes the handsome Burgo as

Burgo Fitzgerald

52. H. K. Browne. *Can You Forgive Her?*

a man whom neither man nor woman could help regarding as a thing beautiful to behold;—but not the less there was there in his eyes and cheeks a look of haggard dissipation—of riotous living, which had become wearisome, by its continuance, even to himself. . . . He became at times pale, sallow, worn, and haggard. He grew thin, and still thinner. . . . But still his beauty remained. (Chapter xxix)

Burgo is, admittedly, a difficult character to depict, But Browne does not really try. Trollope, who in Browne's case peremptorily chose the subjects and saw preliminary drawings,[5] found his inattention to detail infuriating: on the verso of the drawing for this plate is inscribed 'Burgo Fitzgerald wore no beard. See page 142'.[6] (Another feature of Browne's work that may have troubled Trollope was the diminutive scale to which he generally drew his figures.) In the scene illustrated, Burgo, who has been walking the London streets and contemplating running off with Lady Glencora, now Plantagenet Palliser's wife, is accosted by a young and penniless prostitute. Trollope continues:

[Burgo] took her to a public-house and gave her bread and meat and beer, and stood by her while she ate it. She was shy with him then, and would fain have taken it to a corner by herself, had he allowed her. He perceived this, and turned his back to her, but still spoke to her a word or two as she ate. The woman at the bar who served him looked at him wonderingly, staring into his face; and the pot-boy woke himself thoroughly that he might look at Burgo; and the waterman from the cab-stand stared at him; and women who came in for gin looked almost lovingly up into his eyes. He regarded them all not at all, showing no feeling of disgrace at his position, and no desire to carry himself as a ruffler.

Browne has followed the text quite literally, but the drawing suggests a convivial tavern scene from Dickens; for in spite of its would-be seriousness—the sad face of the prostitute—the illustration is too satiric. The passage is intended to show that the villainous Burgo has a good heart and generous impulses; it is typical of Trollope's constant method of being fair to his characters and insisting always on their redeeming qualities. Moreover, as Robert Polhemus has pointed out, Burgo, at the moment he is accosted by the prostitute, is thinking how Glencora has been sold in marriage to Palliser; both women are victims, both are used.[7] The scene

Captain Bellfield proposes a Toast.

53. H. K. Browne. *Can You Forgive Her?*

then is not gratuitous, and Trollope has not chosen it for illustration on a whim. It would be unfair to expect Browne to have captured all the ramifications of the scene, but one might have hoped for something more in keeping with Trollope's purposes. It is nonetheless an animated drawing and one of the most interesting plates in the book.

In the episodes concerning the wealthy widow Greenow and her two suitors, the farmer Cheesacre and Captain Bellfield, Trollope's humour was more broad, more Dickensian than usual, and, accordingly, Browne acquitted himself better in the Greenow episodes than elsewhere in the novel. Moreover, of the twenty subjects Trollope selected for Browne, five are from the Greenow sub-plot, with which scenes Trollope probably thought Browne would be more at home. Reproduced here is 'Captain Bellfield proposes a Toast' (plate 53). In it we see the impecunious Captain getting the edge over the well-to-do but inept farmer, as these two worthies pursue the widow and her money. As in this little skirmish at the beach party, Bellfield, with his touch of romance, will eventually prevail. Browne was especially good at crowded scenes, and this clever arrangement of spirited figures and faces reflects some of his old zest. The caricature, however, is a shade too strong for Trollope's wildest moments of fun. But even in the Greenow illustrations, where Browne is most in his element, he is careless: the widow, for example, looks very different in this plate from that of her first appearance, 'Peace to his Manes' (Chapter vii). (On the other hand, the suitors are recognisable throughout, especially Cheesacre, who bears a family resemblance to Micawber.) Cheesacre in the illustration 'Mrs. Greenow, look at that!' (Chapter xiv), points to what is supposed to be a manure pile but which appears to be hay. And in his final rendering of this group, 'Dear Greenow! dear Husband!' (Chapter xl), Browne has Captain Bellfield and the widow looking at what appears to be a small folding case or locket rather than the book of photographs mentioned in the text.

In *Can You Forgive Her?* Browne attempted two of his so-called 'dark plates'. This process, which Browne began in *Dombey and Son* and brought to considerable perfection in *Bleak House*, involved making numerous close, fine parallel lines which could be bitten in to varying depths. The result was a variation in tone from light grey to velvet-like black. But the two Trollope plates, 'The Priory Ruins' (Chapter xxvii) and 'Swindale Fell' (Chapter xxxi), show none of this gradation of black. Rather, Browne etched every line to a uniform depth and obtained an overall light grey background; the etchings look as if they were printed on grey paper.

'Edgehill' (plate 54), a hunting scene, could have been expected to please Trollope, who was so inordinately devoted to the sport. Browne had something of a reputation for drawing hunting scenes; he had illustrated, for example, Surtees' *Jorrocks' Jaunts and Jollities* and *Hawbuck Grange*. But the Edgehill drawing is not particularly good: although the body of the horse on the right is well drawn, its head and neck appear two-dimensional, as do the other dark horses in the foreground; moreover, the riders of these two horses seem awkwardly mounted. But the overall design effectively suggests movement, beginning with the dogs and horse in the left foreground and continuing counterclockwise through the riderless horse, the tree, branches and clouds. We do not know Trollope's opinion of the drawing; he may have found it rather flippant. Certainly it has little of the grace and elegance Millais gave to his 'Monkton Grange' illustration.

We know that Trollope was unhappy from the start with Browne's drawings. Millais, in a letter dated 13 January 1864—after only one number of *Can You Forgive Her?* had appeared—wrote to his wife:

Hablot Brown[e] is illustrating [Trollope's] new serial. Chapman is publishing it, and [Trollope] is not pleased with the illustrating, and proposed to me to take it off his hands, but I declined. Messrs. C. and H. gave him so much more for his novel [£3000] that they wished to save in the illustrations, and now Trollope is desirous of foregoing his extra price to have it done by me.[8]

These comments are illuminating, especially in view of the sometimes heard but misguided charge that Trollope's chief concern was money. But while his decision to drop Browne evinced a very real sensitivity about the quality of illustration in his novel, the eventual outcome of that decision was not particularly happy. For when Millais continued in his refusal to take up the work, Trollope talked Chapman into hiring one Miss E. Taylor, an amateur of whom nothing is known. At about the time of the switch, Trollope wrote a letter to George Smith, who had suggested Browne as a possible illustrator for *The Claverings*, which was to appear in the *Cornhill*. Trollope said:

I think you would possibly find no worse illustrator than H. Browne; and I think he is almost as bad in one kind as in another. He will take no pains to ascertain the thing to be illustrated. I cannot think that his work can add any value at all to any book.

Edgehill

54. H. K. Browne. *Can You Forgive Her?*

I am having the ten last numbers of Can You Forgive Her illustrated by a lady. She has as yet done two drawings on wood. They are both excellent, and the cutter says that they will come out very well. She has £5:5:—a drawing for them. Why not employ her? She is a Miss Taylor of St. Leonards.

But of course the question is one for you to settle yourself. As for myself I can never express satisfaction at being illustrated in any way by H. Browne.[9]

But if Trollope recognised Browne's ineptitude for illustrating his work, he was not especially astute in his choice of a successor. Miss Taylor may have been a personal friend. Trollope certainly allowed her more freedom in the choice of subjects than he had given Browne:

I intended [he wrote to her] to propose to you to select your own subjects—letting me know what you select before you go to work. As to the numbers which you now have in hand, pray take the single figure you propose.

I now send you two numbers further. I have marked on them some subjects, but have done so as hints—& ask you to use your own judgement.[10]

Trollope said in his letter to Smith that he had seen her first two drawings, and in fairness to him it should be noted that 'Great Jove' (plate 55), the first of these, is among the best of the twenty drawings she was to supply for Can You Forgive Her? It is, oddly enough, the only parliamentary scene—except for one in the late The Way We Live Now—to be illustrated in all of Trollope's fiction. The only palpable fault is the effeminate face of the man to the far right.[11] The drawing is slightly reminiscent of Millais' courtroom scenes for Orley Farm in its arrangement of figures on different levels. The second drawing, ' "Friendships will not come by ordering," said Lady Glencora' (Chapter xlii), is not nearly so good as the first. For one thing, Lady Glencora appears to be extremely shortlegged. But the arrangement of the two figures, one with his back to us, is very much in the manner of Millais, and this no doubt carried weight with Trollope. Whatever Miss Taylor's limitations, she attempted to illustrate in the Millais fashion. There is no caricature here—at least none intended. Her work is stiff, excessively pretty, too serious, but it is not satiric in Browne's fashion. She is a Sixties-style illustrator. One may assume that

Great Jove.

55. E. Taylor. *Can You Forgive Her?*

Lady Glencora.

56. E. Taylor. *Can You Forgive Her?*

Trollope told her to examine Millais' illustrations and to disregard Browne's versions of the very characters she was to pick up in the second half of the novel. She was, predictably, especially poor in the Greenow episodes, which had been Browne's best. In 'Mr. Cheesacre disturbed' (Chapter xlvii), Cheesacre himself is ludicrous. Far better is the illustration titled 'Lady Glencora' (plate 56), which shows Glencora sitting alone before her fireplace, pondering the alternatives of running off with Burgo or staying with her husband. Here the close attention to detail is almost reminiscent of Millais (who would, however, have given much more texture to Glencora's dress). But if this illustration, like her first, does not entirely disappoint, that five pages later, 'Before God, my first wish . . .' is unfortunately more typical of Miss Taylor's work: Glencora is too insignificant-looking for the woman we know her to be. In drawing Plantagenet Palliser the artist may have made some effort to follow up Millais' drawing for *The Small House at Allington*, but Palliser's bird-like eyes, misproportioned left arm, and his casual posture during this dramatic moment—Glencora is telling him she loves Burgo—display all too glaringly Miss Taylor's shortcomings. It is an illustration to make one regret Millais' departure all the more.

Can You Forgive Her? is both a less than distinguished specimen of the art of Victorian book illustration and an oddity. To be sure, in the past various artists had contributed to one book. The famous Moxon *Tennyson*, for example, had been illustrated by many hands and these in turn had represented two very different styles. But the *Tennyson* was of course a collection of poetry; and while one occasionally finds different artists illustrating a single work of fiction—Browne himself had worked with Cattermole on *The Old Curiosity Shop* and *Barnaby Rudge*—they should be artists compatible with each other and whose drawings may be alternated or integrated in some fashion. But in *Can You Forgive Her?* there is a complete break, the first twenty drawings, for Volume I, done in the earlier caricaturist style, the second twenty in a distinctly Sixties manner, however ineptly executed.

A footnote to this atypical episode in the illustration of fiction is found on the title page of the 'Third Edition' of the novel, published by Chapman & Hall in 1866. It reads 'With 40 Illustrations by "Phiz" and Marcus Stone', an error that made it appear that Stone had here supplanted Browne as he had with Dickens. No one seems to have had a good word for Browne at this stage of his career, except, as Michael Sadleir points out,[12] a religious-minded literary crank named J. Hain Friswell, who wrote:

[Trollope's] true pictures of an age very poor and weak in its nature . . . have found an excellent illustrator in a man who has great merit, but which the age persists in accepting as an illustrative artist—you might as well call him a balloonist—John Everett Millais. He is as well fitted to Trollope as Phiz is to Dickens. When Phiz tried to illustrate our author, as he did in 'Can You Forgive Her?', he failed miserably; he absolutely put life and humour into some of the figures under which Trollope had written such subscriptions as these—dry, empty as old nuts, but singularly descriptive of the author and his mind.[13]

As Sadleir concludes, even Friswell seems to have regretted the separation of Millais and Trollope.

MARY ELLEN EDWARDS

The Claverings

The Claverings, the last of the four novels Trollope published in the *Cornhill*, appeared from February 1866 to May 1867. Publisher George Smith wisely declined Trollope's suggestion to employ Miss Taylor for the illustrations, and it would appear that an artist was not settled upon until the last moment. On 21 December 1865 Trollope wrote to Smith:

> I have no doubt that you will do the best in your power as to the illustrations. The book illustrated by Mrs. Edwards has not yet reached me, but as time presses I answer your note at once. . . . I would suggest that the subject for the illustration should be the entrance into the little parish church of Clavering of Lord Ongar with Julia Brabazon as his bride.
>
> Page 24 'A puir feckless thing, tottering along like'. That should be the legend to the picture.
>
> If a vignette be required, as I judge to be your intention, I would propose the two figures of Harry Clavering and Julia Brabazon, where the former stops the latter at the garden gate. Page 1.[1]

Mary Ellen Edwards—'M.E.E.'—(1839–1906) was a prolific and popular illustrator for such publications as *Cassell's Family Magazine*, the *Argosy*, and *Good Words*. For *The Claverings* she supplied sixteen full-page illustrations and sixteen vignettes as the novel appeared in the *Cornhill*; only the full-sized plates were included in the two-volume book edition, published in April 1867.

Trollope said of *The Claverings*:

> I consider the story as a whole to be good, though I am not aware that the public has ever corroborated that verdict. The chief character is that of a young woman [Julia Brabazon Ongar] who has married manifestly for money and rank. . . . Then comes the punishment

A Friendly Talk.

57. M. E. Edwards. *The Claverings*

natural to the offence. When she is free, the man whom she had loved [Harry Clavering] . . . is engaged to another woman. He vacillates and is weak,—in which weakness is the fault of the book.[2]

Trollope organised his plot and sub-plots around Julia Ongar, and while the sixteen illustrations picture almost everyone of any importance to the novel, Julia dominates, appearing in exactly half of the illustrations, including both frontispieces.

In the first illustration, that mentioned in Trollope's letter, and in the second, 'Mr. Saul Proposes' (Chapter vi), Miss Edwards got off to a poor start. In these drawings the men, completely two-dimensional in appearance, look like black cardboard cutouts. The third plate marks a considerable improvement; it shows Lady Ongar, returned from abroad after the death of her husband, speaking with Harry Clavering:

> . . . she was to his eyes so much older than she had been! And yet as he looked at her, he found that she was as handsome as ever,—more handsome than she had ever been before. There was a dignity about her face and figure which became her well, and which she carried as though she knew herself to be in very truth a countess. . . . She seemed to be a woman fitter for womanhood than for girlhood. (Chapter vii)

It is a description to which perhaps subsequent illustrations will do better justice; here, 'A Friendly Talk' (plate 57), she leans pressingly towards Harry and tells him of the indignities she suffered from her late husband. Miss Edwards has caught her earnest, intimate attitude and has given Harry a strained appearance: he seems unwilling to look directly at his former love—he has not told her he is now engaged. The mood suits the text; the details of the room are softened to emphasise the two characters, who are nicely individualised. The rendering of Lady Ongar's dress recalls Millais' manner.

Subsequent illustrations depicting Lady Ongar serve to connect the various sub-plots. For example, in 'Captain Clavering makes his First Attempt' (plate 58), she is seen with Archie Clavering and Sophie Gordeloup. The insincere, rascally, yet not altogether unlikeable Clavering has been encouraged in his hope of marrying the wealthy widow Ongar by his sporting pal, Captain Boodle, with his incessant horseman's metaphor ('Seven thousand a year ain't usually to be picked up merely by trotting easy along the flat . . . this sort of work is very up-hill'; 'Let her know that you're there'—Chapter xvii). Archie is seen here,

CAPTAIN CLAVERING MAKES HIS FIRST ATTEMPT.

58. M. E. Edwards. *The Claverings*

'LADY ONGAR, ARE YOU NOT RATHER NEAR THE EDGE?'

59. M. E. Edwards. *The Claverings*

after having been further fortified by a visit to his hairdresser, 'giving the mare a gallop', i.e. making a first visit to Lady Ongar. But his gallant efforts are interrupted by the unexpected appearance of Madame Sophie Gordeloup, whose interest, like Archie's, is Lady Ongar's money. Sophie is a Franco-Polish woman of fifty, 'a little, dry, bright woman . . . with quick eyes, and thin lips, and small nose, and mean forehead, and scanty hair drawn back quite tightly from her face and head' (Chapter xiii). Miss Edwards has made her perhaps too youthful in appearance (she is older-looking in 'How Damon Parted From Pythias', Chapter xxix), but all three figures are well drawn. Archie's stance brings to mind that which Millais gave Johnny Eames in 'And have I not really loved you?' (plate 33).

In addition to the confused Harry Clavering and the maladroit Archie Clavering, there is still another suitor for Lady Ongar, Count Pateroff. Having obtained information of her whereabouts from his sister, Sophie Gordeloup, Pateroff follows Lady Ongar to the Isle of Wight where he comes upon her unannounced and startles her with the words used as the legend in the illustration, 'Lady Ongar, are you not rather near the edge?' (plate 59). Pateroff appears in clear outline against the sky and sea while the figure of the seated woman almost blends with the rocks. He stands out in the drawing even as he is so unwanted an interruption of her private musings.

In the final illustration of the book, 'Lady Ongar and Florence' (plate 60), Lady Ongar embraces her triumphant rival for Harry Clavering. Miss Edwards has drawn Julia tall and stately, and kept Florence Burton, another of Trollope's 'little brown girls', appropriately shorter. Lady Ongar has dominated until the end; she figured pre-eminently, as we have seen, in both text and illustrations. Indeed, Florence, the nominal heroine, was not illustrated until Chapter xxxii and appeared in only three plates. Her first appearance, 'Florence Burton makes up a Packet' (plate 61), shows her after she heard that Harry had been 'unsteady'; she quickly determines to give him up, but in preparing to return his gifts and letters she takes slow inventory of each article. Miss Edwards' technique here is unusual for a Trollope illustration in that, in an effort to focus altogether on the human subject, there is, aside from a chair and chest, absolutely no pictorial context, no background. One could wish that the artist, less careless of perspective, had put the chair and chest on the same plane. On the other hand, Florence herself is very good. Her face has an attractive if somewhat conventional profile; her figure is well drawn, with strength in her neck and shoulders.

LADY ONGAR AND FLORENCE.

60. M. E. Edwards. *The Claverings*

FLORENCE BURTON MAKES UP A PACKET.

61. M. E. Edwards. *The Claverings*

HARRY SAT BETWEEN THEM, LIKE A SHEEP AS HE WAS, VERY MEEKLY.

62. M. E. Edwards. *The Claverings*

HUSBAND AND WIFE.

63. M. E. Edwards. *The Claverings*

Trollope fell short by making Harry do his duty by the passive Florence. The young man's choice seems to have been dictated to him by his sister, his mother, and Cecilia Burton, a sister-in-law to Florence. In fact, Cecilia, in her efforts on Florence's behalf, has carried on a kind of vicarious love affair with Harry, a facet of the story underlined in the illustration 'Harry sat between them, like a sheep as he was, very meekly' (plate 62). Cecilia sits in the foreground to Harry's right, as dreamily happy with the capture of the vacillating lover as his fiancée, who sits to his left. Harry himself is stiff and his face too much modelled after the Greek ideal.

Quite good are the two plates devoted to Sir Hugh Clavering and his wife Hermione. This simple woman, who is Julia's sister, dotes on her husband, whose constant mistreatment of her parallels the behaviour of Julia's late husband. In the illustration pointedly called 'Husband and Wife' (plate 63), Sir Hugh can hardly bring himself to say goodbye to his wife as he is about to leave on an extended trip. He will be forced to kiss her on the forehead before escaping, 'telling himself, as he went, that she was a fool'. The illustration conveys a sense of suffocation, and his scarcely veiled impatience is perfectly represented. But if Miss Edwards has illustrated Sir Hugh well, Trollope himself disappoints in the end: the contrivance of having both Sir Hugh and Archie drowned, thereby giving to Harry the former's title and lands, is unconvincing and very unlike Trollope's usual avoidance of such twists.

Forrest Reid said Edwards' illustrations for *The Claverings* show her at her best[3] and Gordon Ray speaks of their 'signal merits'.[4] While not in a class with Millais' work, they are a considerable improvement over that for *Can You Forgive Her?* by Browne and Taylor.

GEORGE HOUSMAN THOMAS

The Last Chronicle of Barset

Trollope's practice of carrying over characters from one novel to another presented the challenge of keeping those characters consistent while changing and growing with the years. Literary sequels, often notoriously bad, posed no problem for Trollope; indeed, his Barsetshire and Palliser novels are the best serials in the language. But they presented a problem to his different illustrators, who owed fealty not only to Trollope's text but to previous illustrators. The difficulty first appeared in serious magnitude when Millais declined to do the *Last Chronicle of Barset*. Millais' illustrations for Trollope had been interrupted with *Can You Forgive Her?*, but continuity there had not been a problem except in regard to Plantagenet Palliser, who had been drawn by Millais in *The Small House at Allington*. Furthermore, *The Claverings*, although illustrated by another hand, was an 'independent' work and not connected with either series. But the *Last Chronicle* was to be the summing up of county and church life in this imaginary shire; no one but Millais had drawn for the series, and Trollope did his best to persuade Millais to undertake the work. On 5 August 1866 Trollope wrote to his publisher, George Smith:

> Millais was talking to me about certain illustrations. I said—(after certain other things had been said)—'You know you will not do any more.' He replied—'If you like it I'll do another of yours.' He is in Scotland. Shall I write and ask him?[1]

Trollope then wrote to Millais on 6 August:

> I have written (nearly finished) a story in thirty-two numbers, which is to come out weekly. . . . Smith publishes it, and proposes that there shall be one illustration to every number, with small vignettes to the chapter headings. Will you do them? You said a word to me the other

day, which was to the effect that you would perhaps lend your hand to another story of mine. Many of the characters (indeed, most of them) are people you already know well—Mr. Crawley, Mr. Harding, Lily Dale, Crosbie, John Eam[e]s, and Lady Lufton. George Smith is very anxious that you should consent, and you may imagine that I am equally so. If you can do it, the sheets shall be sent to you as soon as they are printed, and copies of your own illustrations should be sent to refresh your memory.[2]

Trollope followed up with a note on 20 August:

But how about the Illustrations. You promised me a further answer. Do *do* them! They wont take you above half an hour each.[3]

The letters show Trollope's great concern for continuity, but also an ignorance of the methods of Millais, who, although a fast worker, was a perfectionist also.[4] Millais refused, and G. H. Thomas was engaged to provide thirty-two plates and the same number of vignettes for the *Last Chronicle* as it appeared in weekly sixpenny numbers, 1 December 1866 to 6 July 1867. All the illustrations were included in the book edition, two volumes, March and July 1867.

George Housman Thomas (1824–68) was both an engraver and draughtsman on wood (for a time he engraved bank-notes for the U.S. government) as well as a painter, remembered for his oils of ceremonial subjects commissioned by Queen Victoria. His black and white work appeared in such periodicals as the *Illustrated London News* and *London Society*. Along with his drawings for Trollope, his best illustrations were for Wilkie Collins' *Armadale*, which was serialised in the *Cornhill*, 1864–6.

Trollope directed Smith to send copies of *Framley Parsonage* and *The Small House at Allington* to Thomas so that he 'should see the personages as Millais has made them'.[5] Millais' performance was difficult to follow, and Thomas did conscientious but hardly comparable work. We have Trollope's reaction to the first four:

I send back [he wrote to Smith] the proof with the lettering. It is always well if possible to select a subject for which the lettering can be taken from the dialogue. Because this cannot be done as to No. 1 ['Mr. and Mrs. Crawley', Chapter i], the lettering is poor. As to Nos. 2 & 4 ['"I love you as though you were my own," said the Schoolmistress' (plate 64)

"I LOVE YOU AS THOUGH YOU WERE MY OWN," SAID THE SCHOOLMISTRESS.

64. G. H. Thomas. *The Last Chronicle of Barset*

"A Convicted Thief," repeated Mrs. Proudie.

65. G. H. Thomas. *The Last Chronicle of Barset*

and '"A convicted thief," repeated Mrs. Proudie' (plate 65)] – it is all right. In No. 3, the scene is sufficiently distinct to dispense with the rule ['Mr. Crawley before the Magistrates' (plate 66)].

These remarks seem to indicate that Trollope left the choice of subject to Thomas. Trollope continues:

> The best figure is that of Miss Prettyman in No. 2. Grace is not good. She has fat cheeks, & is not Grace Crawley. Crawley before the magistrates is very good. So is the bishop. Mrs. Proudie is not quite my Mrs. Proudie.[6]

Miss Prettyman (plate 64) is indeed delicately drawn, and the close detail of the room very reminiscent of Millais; Grace Crawley does appear fat-cheeked and her face has none of the fine delineation of which Thomas was at times capable. That Trollope should have had to complain that Thomas' Mrs Proudie was 'not quite my Mrs. Proudie' (plate 65) is surely regrettable. Of Trollope's comic characters she is unquestionably supreme, and we should like a rendering of that redoubtable mistress of the Episcopal Palace that agreed with Trollope's conception of her. On the other hand, Trollope calls Thomas' Bishop Proudie 'very good'. Even more fortunately we have representations of Josiah Crawley that coincided with his creator's thinking. Trollope's pleasure in Millais' rendering of Crawley in *Framley Parsonage* (plate 5) has already been mentioned, and now a similar verdict is given Thomas' 'Mr. Crawley before the Magistrates' (plate 66). This drawing, which came to be used as the frontispiece of Volume I of the book edition, has Crawley seen from the back in three-quarter profile; both his stiff pride and self-pitying weariness seem reflected in his outward demeanour. Of the figures around the table, those of the two gentlemen conferring centre are especially good. The entire crowded scene has movement and tension. But Thomas, who drew Crawley in nine full-page illustrations throughout the book, is inconsistent with this central figure. In places Crawley is too young ('Mr. and Mrs. Crawley', Chapter i); elsewhere he is not recognisable ('It's dogged as does it', frontispiece, Volume II). On the other hand, in 'They will come to hear a ruined man declare his own ruin' (plate 67), Crawley, resigned and weary in defeat, is well drawn in what is probably the best illustration in the book. He stands centred in black among a group of his parishioners; all eyes are upon him; the scene has dramatic sense. Thomas, then, was rather successful with Crawley, who is the glory of the novel which Trollope regarded, on the whole, as his best.[7]

MR. CRAWLEY BEFORE THE MAGISTRATES.

66. G. H. Thomas. *The Last Chronicle of Barset*

"THEY WILL COME TO HEAR A RUINED MAN DECLARE HIS OWN RUIN."

67. G. H. Thomas. *The Last Chronicle of Barset*

But if Thomas did fairly well by Crawley, he fell short in many other drawings, producing what must be called uneven and disappointing work. In the *Last Chronicle* Trollope brought together various strands from the five previous Barsetshire novels, and not only had Thomas to pick up characters that Millais had drawn—Mr Harding, Lily Dale, Johnny Eames, Adolphus Crosbie, Squire Dale, Mrs Mary Dale, Mrs Fanny Roberts—but he had also to draw characters never before illustrated and yet long in the public mind: Mrs Proudie, Bishop Proudie, Archdeacon Grantly. Thomas had now, after so many years, to show 'what they really looked like'. With old Mr Harding, for example, whom Millais had drawn so beautifully for *The Small House at Allington*, Thomas fails. His Mr Harding is altogether more conventional and less refined than Millais'. At least twice Thomas has made the old man rather rugged looking—nothing of Millais' delicacy survives. Sometimes Thomas has taken Trollope's text too literally and too carelessly at the same time. Trollope describes Crosbie, carried over from *The Small House at Allington* some few years earlier, as balding and looking much older and much fatter. But Trollope is speaking in comparative terms whereas Thomas has Crosbie appearing as if he could be his rival Eames' grandfather, and at the same time looking quite thin. With the Dale family, Thomas did better work. 'Lily wishes that they might swear to be brother and sister' (plate 68), is another of those painful love scenes wherein Trollope, true to his art, makes Lily persist in her refusal of Eames. The late afternoon shadows, leafless trees and huge stump provide an appropriately sterile atmosphere here. Lily's rigid, upright posture also befits her attitude, and though both faces are somewhat depersonalised and stylised, the drawing has merit.

Thomas was if anything less successful with characters introduced for the first time in the *Last Chronicle* and altogether his own pictorialisations. Mr Toogood, for example, looks utterly different in his various appearances. With the so-called London scenes, those extraneous episodes that many readers and critics believe to have damaged Trollope's masterpiece, Thomas has, so to speak, followed suit. The four attendant illustrations are probably the poorest in the book.

Thomas was on the whole unequal to the task of following Trollope as he brought to an end his saga of Barsetshire. Reid called Thomas' illustrations for the *Last Chronicle* 'conscientious work, by no means devoid of merit, though they rarely attain beauty, and are not free from a certain coarseness of touch'.[8] And Sadleir claimed (either by his own

LILY WISHES THAT THEY MIGHT SWEAR TO BE BROTHER AND SISTER.

68. G. H. Thomas. *The Last Chronicle of Barset*

judgment or from some evidence that has not survived) that the 'comparative failure of G. H. Thomas to interpret the characters as their creator saw them, helped to kill Trollope's interest in his illustrators',[9] an assertion which, aside from Trollope's having engaged Millais for *Phineas Finn*, is quite accurate.

MARCUS STONE

He Knew He Was Right

Among illustrations for Trollope novels, first rank after Millais' must be awarded to Marcus Stone's drawings for *He Knew He Was Right*. The novel appeared in thirty-two sixpenny weekly parts from 17 October 1868 to 22 May 1869, each number containing one full-page illustration and one vignette chapter heading, all of which were included in the first book edition, in two volumes, May 1869. Marcus Stone (1840–1921) was not primarily an illustrator, and in the 1870s he devoted himself entirely to painting; in 1877 he became an Associate of the Royal Academy and ten years later a full Academician. During the 1860s Stone had drawn for the *Cornhill*, *Good Words* and other periodicals. In 1864 he had supplied a very unremarkable frontispiece for the cheap edition of Trollope's *Tales of All Countries*. But owing to Dickens' enormous popularity and the practice of preserving in subsequent editions the original illustrations, Stone is chiefly remembered as the illustrator of *Our Mutual Friend* (1864–5). Stone claimed that he had been handicapped by Dickens' 'harassing restrictions' and added that he regarded these early efforts in black and white as 'very immature'.[1] Five years later, when he illustrated *He Knew He Was Right*, Stone was more sure of his drawing and the wood-engraving medium. Reid, with good reason, called Stone's illustrations for Trollope 'probably the best he ever made'[2] and Sadleir called them the only relief from the decadence of later illustrations to Trollope.[3] On the other hand, Q. D. Leavis thinks that Stone 'threw away his opportunities in illustrating Trollope's wide-ranging and interesting novel ... Stone apparently having no conception of what illustrating a novel meant'.[4] Trollope himself had some objections to Stone's work. James Virtue, publisher of the novel in its part-issue, wrote to Trollope in March 1869:

> This time of the year is always bad for Artists work, in the way of book Illustrations—they only think of their Academy pictures and

everything else is dismissed with scant attention—I shall see Stone in a few days—but he has now so nearly finished the whole book that it will not perhaps be worth while to object strongly.[5]

The nature or extent of Trollope's displeasure with Stone is unknown, but we do have Trollope's verdict on his own work in *He Knew He Was Right*, and his assessment is a good example of an author's faulty judgment of his own writing:

> I do not know that in any literary effort I ever fell more completely short of my own intention. . . . It was my purpose to create sympathy for the unfortunate [Louis Trevelyan] who, while endeavouring to do his duty to all around him, should be led constantly astray by his unwillingness to submit his own judgement to the opinion of others. The man is made to be unfortunate enough . . . but the sympathy has not been created yet. I look upon the story as being nearly altogether bad.[6]

Modern criticism has disagreed, almost unanimously, with this appraisal, and one could do no better on this score than to quote Henry James:

> [Trollope] often achieved a conspicuous intensity of the tragical. The long, slow process of the conjugal wreck of Louis Trevelyan and his wife (in *He Knew He Was Right*) . . . arrives at last at an impressive completeness of misery. It is the history of an accidental rupture between two stiff-necked and ungracious people—'the little rift within the lute'—which widens at last into a gulf of anguish. Touch is added to touch, one small, stupid, fatal aggravation to another; and as we gaze into the widening breach we wonder at the vulgar materials of which tragedy sometimes composes itself. I have always remembered the chapter called 'Casalunga,' towards the close of *He Knew He Was Right*, as a powerful picture of the insanity of stiff-neckedness. Louis Trevelyan, separated from his wife, alone, haggard, suspicious, unshaven, undressed, living in a desolate villa on a hill-top near Siena and returning doggedly to his fancied wrong, which he has nursed until it becomes an hallucination, is a picture worthy of Balzac. Here and in several other places Trollope has dared to be thoroughly logical; he has not sacrificed to conventional optimism; he has not been afraid of a misery which should be too much like life.[7]

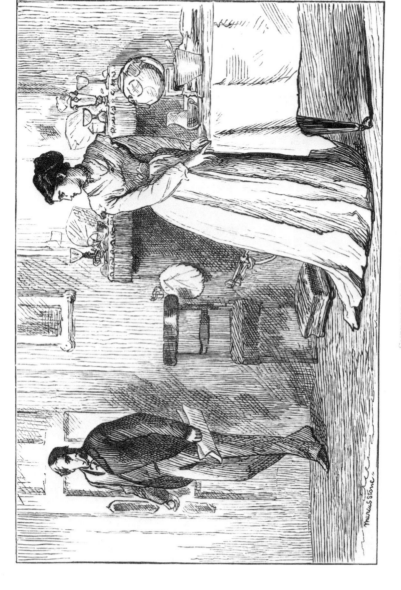

69. M. Stone. *He Knew He Was Right*

70. M. Stone. *He Knew He Was Right*

The 'accidental rupture' in the marriage of Louis and Emily Trevelyan is occasioned by visits paid to the wife by an old friend of her family, one Colonel Osborne, a fifty-year-old bachelor with a reputation as a philanderer. Trevelyan's objections rouse his wife to indignation. Stone's drawings of the unfortunate couple take up with answering illustrations, 'Shewing how wrath began' (plate 69) and 'Shewing how reconciliation was made' (plate 70). Of the two illustrations, the first is superior, except that Trevelyan looks entirely too old—he is but twenty-six or twenty-seven at the time. The drawing exemplifies Stone's work and differentiates it from Millais'. Stone's style is drier, more nervous, more dramatic. He creates naturalness of expression and pose, and is adept at catching movement. Trevelyan and his wife are clearly eye to eye, yet pulling apart. The distance between them is very real. Trevelyan's posture at the door is perfectly rendered; one can almost hear the doorknob turn in his hand. Stone is more economic of line in his central figures than Millais, and he will often do little more than hint at background items such as furniture.

The reconciliation of husband and wife is short-lived. Trevelyan, angered at what he considers his wife's disobedience in refusing to turn Osborne away, gradually comes to the obsessive belief that she has been unfaithful. The two separate, and he falls victim to a powerful monomania; their son becomes a source of still deeper alienation as Trevelyan abducts the child from its mother. In Stone's last illustration of the estranged pair, 'It is hard to speak sometimes' (plate 71), the child is present, looking on as husband and wife come to painful near embrace. Stone just manages to avoid excessive sentimentality. The final drawing of the husband, who at this point has become patently unbalanced, is 'Trevelyan at Casalunga' (plate 72). In this powerful illustration we see a lonely man, rendered in almost solid black, seated brooding upon a rock, his body grown thin, his face emaciated, his hair dishevelled. Set against a Tuscan landscape of cypress and olive trees, Trevelyan seems a Byronic figure.

Of course all could not be gloom in a Trollope novel, at least not in one this long, and Stone supplied some good illustrations in connection with the various love matches. For example, 'The Rivals' (plate 73), representing Nora Rawley and Caroline Spalding, shows much of the refinement and elegance we associate with Millais' drawing-room scenes. On the other hand, the drawing is typical of Stone's best manner, a few lines doing considerable service, the subjects relaxed and natural.

It is hard to speak sometimes.

71. M. Stone. *He Knew He Was Right*

TREVELYAN AT CASALUNGA.

72. M. Stone. *He Knew He Was Right*

THE RIVALS.

73. M. Stone. *He Knew He Was Right*

Another illustration, 'And why does he come here?' (plate 74), depicting the Rawley Family—old Sir Marmaduke is objecting to Hugh Stanbury, Nora's suitor—demonstrates Stone's powers of composition: the family is framed by the swirl of Emily's black dress toward the centre from the left and by that of Nora's white dress from the other side. Marmaduke is clearly talking with Emily, and though Nora's back is turned, we can sense that what he is saying is very painful to her. The figures are somewhat smaller than Millais', yet larger than Browne's. As in this illustration, Stone's scale often gives the appearance of a theatre stage setting.

At the same time, Stone shows himself capable of idyllic outdoor scenes, as in the final illustration of the book, 'Monkhams' (plate 75). This drawing depicts Nora and Hugh Stanbury seated under a hollow old oak at the immense country seat of Charles Glascock, now Lord Peterborough. The grandeur of the estate is enhanced by a glimpse of the great house itself in the extreme background. Nora, engaged now to Stanbury, who is a newspaper writer, would have been mistress of Glascock's wealth had she accepted him, a fact of which she is wistfully but not regretfully aware. To have Nora and Stanbury visit Monkhams near the end of the story was a fine touch on Trollope's part, and by choosing to have the scene illustrated the author (or artist) has underscored this fact very well. Stone, by drawing the lovers very small, has emphasised the grand estate that the young lady has forfeited. The illustration makes its point in delicate and subtle fashion.

Even more than the love affairs of Nora Rawley and Caroline Spalding, the escapades revolving around old Miss Jemima Stanbury provide contrast, indeed comic relief, to the sombre story of Trevelyan's journey into madness and death. Trollope himself saw the novel 'in part redeemed by certain scenes in the house and vicinity of an old maid in Exeter'.[8] Clever-tongued Aunt Jemima is one of the best examples of a familiar literary breed, the benign despot. In 'Aunt Stanbury at dinner will not speak' (plate 76) she has just quarrelled with her niece, whose brother Hugh she accused of selling himself by writing 'sedition' for a penny newspaper. Stone has followed closely Trollope's description of the old lady: her 'strong Roman nose . . . thin lips, and sharp-cut chin' are plainly visible; her stiff upright posture and dark dress seem perfectly correct. Her niece, by contrast, is less rigid and dressed in white. Two attendants enhance the comicality of the scene: the servant, looking supercilious and standing with folded arms to the left of Aunt Stanbury, and a white cat, assuming a remarkably similar sentry-like posture to the left of Dorothy.

"AND WHY DOES HE COME HERE?"

74. M. Stone. *He Knew He Was Right*

MONKHAMS.

75. M. Stone. *He Knew He Was Right*

AUNT STANBURY AT DINNER WILL NOT SPEAK.

76. M. Stone. *He Knew He Was Right*

The comic-relief Exeter scenes of Miss Stanbury and her circle include the affairs of Mr Gibson, the bungling clergyman she had unsuccessfully tried to match in marriage with her niece. Gibson is hotly pursued by two sisters, Arabella and Camilla French, and in the illustration 'I wonder why people make these reports' (plate 77) Arabella is wrenching from him a declaration that there is nothing in the rumour that he is engaged to Dorothy Stanbury, when in fact he is under promise to Aunt Stanbury to ask for Dorothy's hand the very next day. Again Stone follows his practice of contrasting light and dark apparel for his two central figures, using parallel lines rather than cross-hatching to achieve the darkened areas, and but lightly suggesting background figures. Arabella's chignon, which will play an important role as the story progresses, is appropriately prominent. Gibson's face, slightly haughty, as if superior to such idle talk, is funny but not overly caricatured.

The vignettes that Stone drew for the beginning of each part-issue merit consideration.[9] Not only are Stone's vignettes good, they were reproduced in the book edition. (In contrast, Millais' vignettes for *The Small House at Allington*, superior certainly to Stone's, were unfortunately not included in the book publication.)[10] The vignette, in addition to making the page attractive, serves also to show the alert reader of the book edition how the author had allocated his materials to fit part-issue. And, of course, these small drawings illustrate the text in a number of ways corroborative of the larger plates. The vignettes are occasionally used when a character first appears, as a kind of introductory portrait, such as that found at the beginning of Chapter vii, 'Miss Jemima Stanbury of Exeter'. This vignette (plate 78, upper left) delineates Aunt Stanbury's features very carefully, and Stone keeps subsequent representations of the character consistent with this first (compare plate 76). In this vignette Stone has closely followed the description given in the text. In others, Stone has allowed himself a larger interpretative role, as in that to Chapter iv, 'Hugh Stanbury', where the vignette shows that gentleman wigged as barrister but asleep during a court session. Trollope's text merely indicates that Stanbury sat idle in court and never made a guinea during his four years as a barrister. Again, in his vignette of the Clock House (plate 78, lower left), Stone uses his imagination in fashioning a small illustration of that house— important in the story as the place where Osborne once again foolishly visited Emily Trevelyan after she had separated from her husband and where Nora had earlier refused Glascock—but of which house Trollope offers practically no description. Other vignettes illustrate precise dramatic

"I WONDER WHY PEOPLE MAKE THESE REPORTS."

77. M. Stone. *He Knew He Was Right*

78. M. Stone. Four vignettes. Capitals for Chapters vii, x, xiii and xlvii, *He Knew He Was Right*

moments of the story, such as that showing Trevelyan in the hall of his house picking up Emily's note to Colonel Osborne (plate 78, upper right), or that of the Reverend Mr Gibson, at tea with Arabella French and becoming suddenly so horrified at her chignon (plate 78, lower right). Finally, some vignettes illustrate characters prominent in the text but never included in a plate, such as Mr Charles Glascock, the future Lord Peterborough, shown with Trevelyan at the beginning of Chapter xxxvii, or the less important but interesting Miss Wallachia Petrie, 'The Republican Browning', in the vignette to Chapter lxxxi.

DECADENCE

As the 1860s drew to a close the quality in English black-and-white illustrations declined. Even Millais was not on top form towards the end of the decade. But Trollope on the whole had been very fortunate during the 'golden' years: Millais had collaborated superbly on four novels, and Marcus Stone and M. E. Edwards had each contributed creditable performances. Less successful, but not to be despised, was the work of G. H. Thomas for the *Last Chronicle*. The only substantial failure had been the drawings of Browne and Miss Taylor for *Can You Forgive Her?* But if the 1860s had in the main provided Trollope's fiction with effective illustration, the close of the decade and the beginning of the next produced illustrations that can only be said to mar his books. Not enough evidence remains to establish the degree to which Trollope became resigned and indifferent in the matter of illustration; we simply do not know how active a role he played with regard to the drawings for *The Vicar of Bullhampton*, *Ralph the Heir*, *Phineas Redux*, and *The Way We Live Now*.

The Vicar of Bullhampton had been scheduled for publication in *Once A Week*, but Bradbury & Evans, publishers of the magazine, had purchased the rights to a new Victor Hugo novel which, because of the author's 'incessant corrections', was delayed until it would have run side by side with Trollope's novel. Trollope wrathfully declined to have his story appear in another and less important of the firm's publications, the *Gentleman's Magazine*, and Bradbury & Evans published *The Vicar of Bullhampton* in twelve shilling numbers, from July 1869 to May 1870. The illustrations, twenty-three plates and twelve vignettes, all of which were included in the book edition, April 1870, were by the relatively unknown Henry Woods (1846–1921), a painter who in 1876 moved permanently to Venice where he painted genre scenes of that city. Little known as an illustrator, he is not mentioned by either White or Reid. Most of Woods' drawings for Trollope are inept, the figures squat, the faces peculiar. *The Vicar of Bullhampton*, Trollope said in his *Autobiography*, was written 'chiefly with the object of exciting not only pity but sympathy for a fallen woman',[1] but the drawings of the woman, Carry Brattle, are especially poor. A contemporary reviewer remarked: 'Mr. Trollope cannot be reproached with making vice attractive. He tells us that Carry is pretty—an impression of which the illustrator has done his best to disabuse us.'[2] It is noteworthy that the authorised American publisher of the novel, Lippincott, did not reproduce or copy the original plates, as American publishers almost invariably did, but instead had entirely new illustrations supplied.

After Millais completed *Phineas Finn*, F. A. Fraser (and others) took up the illustration of Trollope's *St Paul's Magazine*—although Fraser's name would never appear on the magazine cover as had Millais'. Francis Arthur Fraser was a decidedly minor but prolific illustrator of the late 1860s and the 1870s. He had, for example, singlehandedly done most of the illustrations for *Good Words* for 1869. Fraser drew eighteen plates for *Ralph the Heir*, a novel with a most extraordinarily involved publication history. It appeared in nineteen sixpenny monthy parts from January 1870 to July 1871, all except the last number having one full-page illustration by Fraser. Simultaneously it was issued in the unusual form of a free supplement sewn in at the back of *St Paul's Magazine* for the same months, but without some of the illustrations. Both part-issues were under the Strahan imprint. The first book edition, published in three volumes by Hurst & Blackett, appeared in April 1871 with no illustrations. About two months later, Strahan followed with a one-volume edition with eleven of the original illustrations, and in the following year Routledge published a one-volume cheap edition with all eighteen plates.[3] Fraser's drawings, though better than Woods', are not memorable. They have no proper legends, merely the words 'Ralph the Heir',—whatever the subject of the drawing. This kind of sloppiness seems to indicate a very real lack of concern on Trollope's part.

Fraser took part in a later venture of Trollope's, the eight-volume *Chronicles of Barsetshire*, published by Chapman & Hall in 1878. In April of that year Trollope wrote to Millais:

I am bringing out a series of six novels to be called the Chronicles of Barsetshire. Framley Parsonage will be one. I want some good young artist to do a frontispiece for each;—but am very anxious to have them well done as we mean to have the six volumes as nice as we can make them. If he would do six nice coloured drawing[s] Chapman would pay him. Whom could you recommend to me?[4]

" It's dogged as does it."—p. 201

79. F. A. Fraser. *The Last Chronicle of Barset*

Anyone ignorant of Trollope's straightforward manner might be tempted to think Trollope was hinting for Millais to do the drawings himself. In any event, F. A. Fraser, who can hardly be seen as someone newly recommended by Millais, drew eight frontispieces for the series. None is exceptional, but that for the second volume of the *Last Chronicle* is of some interest because the subject and legend are identical with the frontispiece of Volume II of the original issue as drawn by G. H. Thomas. Crawley and Giles Hoggett, the brickmaker from Hoggle End, stand in the rain as the latter gives his troubled pastor the homely advice, 'It's dogged as does it.' In neither illustration does the clergyman resemble Millais' Crawley, or, for that matter, Crawley as Thomas drew him elsewhere, but Fraser's version (plate 79) is to be preferred to Thomas'. The driving rain, the mud, and the wet sheen reflecting the human figures all contribute to create an environmental gloom that adumbrates Crawley's state of mind. The plate is in some ways a sophisticated work and one that owes much to the talent of the engraver.

Phineas Redux, fourth of the Palliser series (the third and last to be illustrated) appeared weekly in the *Graphic* from 19 July 1873 to 10 January 1874. The twenty-six illustrations, twenty-four of which were included in the book edition, were by Francis Montague Holl (1845–88), a young painter who began his career as a 'social realist', drawing the poor, and who later turned to portraiture. Most of his illustrations were produced for the *Graphic*. The significance of this weekly to the illustration of the 1870s (and to Trollope's later fiction) cannot be overestimated. All of Trollope's illustrators during this later period, including Woods and Fraser, drew in the *Graphic* style; indeed Woods often drew for the *Graphic* in its first years. This magazine, founded by William L. Thomas (brother of G. H. Thomas), was intended to rival the *Illustrated London News*. According to White, the *Graphic* 'revolutionised English illustration. . . . Its influence for good or ill was enormous. With its first number, published on December 4, 1869, we find a definite, official date to close the record of the "sixties".'[5] The most important figure of the 'Graphic School' was William Small, who began as a Sixties illustrator, contributing to such magazines as *Good Words*, the *Argosy*, and *Once A Week*. Reid's judgment is harsh: Small's new manner, having begun in the 1860s, came into its own in the *Graphic* where, 'apart altogether from the substitution of "wash" for "line"—in itself a sufficiently disastrous innovation—the old ideal has disappeared: art is turning to journalism, beauty to prettiness, sentiment to sentimentality, the work is planned from the beginning to appeal to a larger and less cultured public.'[6] (Ruskin termed the new style 'Blottesque'.)[7] Small was to illustrate Trollope's *Marian Fay* as it appeared serially in the *Graphic* from 3 December 1881 to 3 June 1882. None of these execrable drawings was reproduced in the book edition. In addition, two short Trollope fictions were illustrated as they were brought out in the *Graphic* during the seventies: *Harry Heathcote of Gangoil*, published in the Christmas number for 1873 with six illustrations by various artists, none of which was included in the first book edition (although they appeared, reduced in size,[8] in the second edition), and *Christmas at Thompson Hall*, published in the Christmas number for 1876, with eight illustrations, all of which were reproduced in facsimile in Harper's (American) edition. The illustrations for these three *Graphic* stories are beneath contempt. Holl's illustrations, whatever their limitations, are at least superior to these later efforts.

Phineas Redux represented the second half of what with *Phineas Finn* was one novel, in spite of the almost six years which intervened between the first instalment of each. But *Phineas Redux* is in some ways quite different from the earlier work: *Redux* is distinctly more political, more sensational, and, on the whole, more sombre. Between the writing of *Phineas Finn* and *Phineas Redux* Trollope had been defeated by dishonest election practices in his bid to sit in Parliament for Beverley[9] and had seen the failure of *St Paul's Magazine*. Whether or not these personal disappointments were in any way contributing factors, *Phineas Redux* is far more pessimistic than *Phineas Finn*. A glance at the plates, even by one unfamiliar with the story, reveals a prevailing gloom: agonised men and women, death scenes, captions telling of murder and fear of execution. Moreover, many of the plates themselves are overwhelmingly black. But drawings of pathetic-looking people and illustrations literally dark were insufficient to accomplish a difficult task. For here again was a large group of characters once drawn by Millais and now the responsibility of an inferior talent: Phineas himself, Lady Laura Kennedy, Madame Max Goesler, Lady Glencora, Plantagenet Palliser, the old Duke of Omnium, Lord and Lady Chiltern. Holl's Phineas, for example, who appears in nine illustrations, is not the handsome young man Millais had depicted. Of course he is supposed to look older, but only two fictional years have passed since Phineas returned to Ireland at the close of the earlier novel. As Holl drew him, Phineas seems to have lost all his dash and verve, and this before the devastation of his being mistakenly accused and tried for murder. Even more unhappily, Holl has overstated the changes that suffering has wrought upon Lady Laura. Holl's interpretation would be acceptable had he not taken Trollope too literally, or rather, rendered too literally Lady Laura's own thoughts about herself. The text for 'Lady Laura at the Glass' (plate 80) speaks of Laura seeing herself as an old woman with nothing of life left but its dregs. But whatever her thoughts, she is scarcely past thirty and ought not to appear well past fifty. But aside from this misreading, the illustration is far superior to most in the novel.

With the forty full-page plates that accompanied the twenty monthly parts in which *The Way We Live Now* appeared from February 1874 to September 1875, the absolute nadir of illustration in the Trollope canon is reached. For many years it was customary to hold Luke Fildes responsible for these despicable drawings; authorities of no less stature than Reid, Sadleir, and Booth perpetuated the error. Certainly one can regret that Fildes, an able illustrator best remembered today for his drawings for Dickens' *The Mystery of Edwin Drood*, was not called upon to do *The Way We Live Now*, one of Trollope's most highly regarded works. That Fildes, whose full name was Samuel Luke Fildes, had not done so should have been obvious from the very clear initials 'LGF' on the drawings. The illustrations were by one Lionel Grimston Fawkes (1849–1931), of the Royal Artillery, an amateur whose only other effort at book illustration was for his aunt's *The Washburn and Other Poems* (1879).[10] None of the illustrations for *The Way We Live Now* is reproduced here, but all forty plates were included in the first and second book editions and therein can be seen stiff awkward figures, ugly faces, contorted limbs, paw-like hands, and mongoloid-looking children. The drawings are in fact poorly executed imitations of the *Graphic* style.

And what of Trollope at this time? He had apparently thrown up his hands in despair over the whole problem of illustration. In a letter written 1 May 1874, while *The Way We Live Now* was appearing in shilling numbers, Trollope said to Mary Holmes:

What you say of illustrations is all true,—not strong enough in expression of disgust. But what can a writer do? I desire, of course, to put my books into as many hands as possible, and I take the best mode of doing so.[11]

An honest and disconcerting note this, and a far cry from the early letters touching Millais' illustrations or the undiluted praise given that artist in the *Autobiography*. It would seem that after the loss of Millais, Trollope

LADY LAURA AT THE GLASS.

80. F. Holl. *Phineas Redux*

81. Original wash drawing for 'Lady Laura at the Glass'

would have preferred not to have had his books illustrated, at least not by the illustrators available.

Both the delight in Millais and the displeasure with his later illustrators came from a man who, whatever self-disparagement he affected in these matters, prided himself on his knowledge of art. Trollope is sometimes thought of as somewhat philistine, a thoroughly John Bullish Briton who happened to have a gift for dashing off very readable stories. The truth is that Trollope had fairly wide-ranging intellectual interests, and among these art was very much to the fore. In 1875, while visiting his son in Australia, Trollope wrote to Millais: 'The one thing I regret most at being absent from England is not seeing the pictures'[12]—a reference to the annual Summer Exhibition at the Royal Academy. (It was fitting that W. P. Frith painted Trollope so conspicuously in *The Private View of the Royal Academy, 1881*.)[13] Trollope wrote three fairly elaborate statements on art: the final chapter of *The New Zealander* (1856), 'The National Gallery' (1861), an article originally intended as a lecture, and 'The Art Tourist' (1865), an article later reprinted in *Travelling Sketches*. All three reveal an inveterate museum-visitor, one widely exposed to art, a man with easily recognisable Victorian preferences—such as that for 'subject' paintings, works that 'tell a story'—and an observer who mixed perceptive and wrongheaded judgments. He will defend, for example, the excellence of Hogarth, but in the same sentence give equal praise to David Wilkie; he will bracket Richard Wilson and A. W. Callcott with Reynolds. He will on the one hand utter platitudes such as the remark that Bellini's portrait of the Doge Loredano 'will not probably attract your attention if you merely pass it; but if you will stand over it and look into it, you will almost wonder that the old man should be so life-like and yet not speak to you'. On the other hand Trollope could write provocatively that

[Raphael] was no doubt a wonderful artist; but in nothing so wonderful as in this, that having reached the top of the tree himself in his very short life, he prepared absolute ruin for all who were to come after him. After him, sharp upon his death, there came ruin and decay, and hideous abortions,—that ruin which will always attend departure from truth. Raphael's grace had been the grace of fiction, and not the grace of nature. The artists of Italy were stricken with wonder, and followed the falsehood faithfully, without attaining the grace. It was he and Michael Angelo, between them, who did the mischief.[14]

These observations are from the 1861 article on the National Gallery; four years later in 'The Art Tourist' Trollope said that as the student of art becomes more familiar with his subject he will come to see how 'those long-visaged, fair-haired virgins [of Botticelli] grew out of the first attempts at female dignity by Cimabue, and how they progressed into the unnatural grace of Raphael, and then descended into the meretricious inanities of which Raphael's power and Raphael's falseness were the forerunners'.[15] One wonders if Trollope heard this sort of talk from Millais. In any case, his comments are perspicacious enough at one point, distinctly commonplace at another, even as his appreciation of Millais' talent as his illustrator could exist side by side with his at least apparent satisfaction in the less than mediocre work of Miss Taylor. In art criticism Trollope was a hard-working amateur, possessed of both the enthusiasms and liabilities common to that status.

ARTIST AND ENGRAVER

An illustrator's work must be judged by its appearance in print. Nevertheless, because the drawings of Millais and other illustrators of Trollope were engraved, indeed interpreted, by other hands, one is anxious to see how well the engraver has 'translated' the original drawings to the wood. But a just comparison requires that some rudimentary facts of the process be borne in mind. Wood engraving differs from both steel and copper engraving and from the older wood cutting. The wood engraver, while using the traditional graver or burin of the metal engraver, cuts away that portion of the surface which is not to be printed—the white areas; wood engraving is thus called 'white line' engraving. The cutter leaves raised those portions of the block that are to take ink and appear in black; thus a wood block is printed in relief, as is letterpress. On the other hand, the copper or steel engraver cuts into the metal lines that are to appear in black; ink is forced into the grooves, and the illustration is produced by intaglio printing rather than by relief printing. Etching, which requires intaglio printing also, was often combined with engraving; in Victorian times plates called 'engravings on steel' were often in fact etchings. Wood engraving differs from wood cutting in that the former is done with engraver's tools on the end grain of very hard wood such as boxwood; wood cutting is worked with a knife or gouge on the plank side of a relatively soft wood such as pear. An often neglected though relevant technical point about Sixties illustrations is made clear in the preface to a folio collection of plates called *The Cornhill Gallery* (1864): 'The impressions of the Pictures which have appeared in the various numbers of *The Cornhill Magazine* were unavoidably subject to the disadvantage of being printed from electrotype casts taken from the Wood-blocks, and with the great speed necessary to insure the punctual publication of a Periodical Work which enjoys the favour of a very large circulation. *The Wood-blocks themselves have now been printed from for the first time*, in the production of *The Cornhill Gallery*.' That the Trollope illustrations were printed from electrotype casts is disconcerting until one compares them with the impressions made directly from the wood blocks. The latter sometimes appear ever so slightly darker and sharper, but those from the electrotypes are remarkably similar in quality.[1]

It is not always possible to determine how accurately the engraver has rendered the artist's drawing in wood because the original sometimes existed only in the pencil drawing on the wood block and was of course destroyed during the engraving process. However, in many instances enough materials remain to provide a fairly telling comparison of what the artists intended and what the engravers produced. The drawing may exist in various early and later stages, and in Millais' case, sufficient examples survive to reveal not only his original intention but his working habits as well. There are, for example, embryonic preliminary sketches that doubtless served in working out an overall design, such as those reproduced here for the *Orley Farm* illustration 'Over their Wine' (plate 22; compare 21). Of much more help are 'original' drawings, such as that reproduced here of Lord Lufton and Lucy Robarts, Millais' very first illustration for Trollope (plate 2). It will be noted that this pencil drawing is in the same orientation as the printed plate, and that the artist had to copy or trace the drawing in reverse onto the wood block. A comparison of this drawing with the illustration (plate 1) demonstrates the extraordinary ability of the engravers (here as so often for Millais, the Dalziel brothers); indeed, in this instance, the print is if anything more delicate, especially in the depiction of Lucy's face. Of course Millais himself transferred the drawing to the block and he may have improved upon the 'original' while so doing; in fact, he may have regarded the pencil drawing as somewhat tentative. But the print and the drawing are surprisingly close in detail and feeling, although there is no one-to-one identification of line. That Millais worked very much with the engraver in mind is evident. The original is a line drawing with a minimum of light and dark pencilling; for where the artist resorts to shading and solid grey areas the engraver must interpret these in line. But here most of the parallel lines and cross-hatching are Millais'.[2] For this illustration the wood block itself survives (plate 82) in the Hartley Collection of the Boston Museum of Fine Arts, as does yet another pencil drawing, the latter in so finished a state as to suggest it may have been done after the engraved version.

Early in the 1860s the Dalziels began the practice, before engraving, of taking a photograph of the pencil drawing that had been made on the wood block. Reproduced here is one such photograph, that for the illustration 'And have I not really loved you?' (plate 34). (The drawing is

82. Wood block for 'Lord Lufton and Lucy Robarts' (compare plate 1)

reversed, and the engraver's name, which in the finished print will receive equal prominence with the artist's monogram, is of course not yet present.) Such a photograph is especially helpful for it shows precisely what Millais presented to the engraver and provides a more reliable criterion by which to judge the engraver's work than does the 'original' pencil drawing. Again the likeness to the finished print (plate 33) is remarkable, although here the original is clearly superior in certain details, notably in the delicacy of the heroine's face. A *preliminary* pencil drawing (also in reverse orientation) for this illustration is preserved in the Taylor Collection. It too is more delicate than the engraved plate, though less so than the subsequent drawing made directly on the wood.

An illustration can also exist in a later version either drawn or painted from the original design or print. Reproduced here is a later rendering of the celebrated 'Was it not a lie?' (plate 4), dated 1861, one year after the print. This pen-and-ink and watercolour drawing is markedly superior to the wood engraving; the face is that of a real woman whereas by comparison that of the print resembles a figurine; the later version also captures the stiffness of the crinoline dress in a way the wood engraving could not. (The subject of a young woman dissolved in tears upon her bed seems to have been a favourite for Millais: remarkably similar to the Trollope illustration except for the plain dress is a drawing [plate 83]³ dating probably from 1854 and intended to illustrate the lines from *In Memoriam*:

> Like some poor girl whose heart is set
> On one whose rank exceeds her own.
>
> At night she weeps, 'How vain am I!
> How should he love a thing so low?'

See also Millais' first drawing for the Moxon *Tennyson*, 'Mariana' [1857] and his first for *Once A Week*, 'Magenta' [2 July 1859].) Attention has already been drawn to another and beautiful watercolour version of an illustration, that of 'Rachel Ray' (plate 43).

Still another state of the illustration, some fine examples of which have survived, is the 'touched proof'. When an engraving had been cut, a burnished proof on India paper was sent to the artist for corrections. In the proof reproduced here, 'Peregrine's Eloquence' (plate 11), Millais has made comments and corrective sketches in the margins and 'touched' the

83. J. E. Millais. Pen-and-ink and grey wash drawing

print itself with Chinese white. With reference to the figure of Lady Mason, for example, he wrote: 'You have cut the looking down lids too straight . . . cut away the two outer coils of hair . . . the nose too much cut in on left side . . . mouth too long cut from the left makes it appear large— . . . get the face *as much like what it is now* as possible. I have lightened the chin & cut the light side of the mouth to make it less long. Compare this proof with another untouched—This cut can be much improved—Let me have another corrected proof *mind*.'[4] These are the comments of a perfectionist. The changes are minute but important, and can be seen only by a very close comparison of the proof with the finished illustration (plate 10); no uncorrected proof survives, or the comparison would be more easily made.

In another instance, namely the drawing of Lady Lufton and the Duke of Omnium for *Framley Parsonage*, Millais sent Dalziel a letter of directions interspersed with sketches:

> Miss Dunstables mouth wants clearing between the nose & upperlip, & you may make her skirt broader by cutting away some of the little lines—Miss Grantleys profile also wants a touch—the line of the forehead going into the nose [sketch] is too thick, cut away from the inside, & cut away the lines crossing her dress on her bosom [sketch] also lighten her hand, the glove—the upper part—Cut away more of the lines of Lady Lufton's headdress [sketch] make it broader. Also the back lady's chin & throat line require fining [sketch]. The mustached man to the right, his forehead, & nose [sketch] make one fine line instead of the thick one—Don't you think the illustration sh^d be without the line round it to go with the others which were without, make it light round Lady Lufton's head, & cut away this [sketch] so as to relieve her head more— I hope you will be able to do these little alterations as I know they will improve it immensely— Sh^d it be in the printers hands still I hope you will be able to do these touches.[5]

Unfortunately, there was not time, and the corrections were not made, as an inspection of the print (plate 6) readily shows.

Sometime during the 1860s there was perfected a technique whereby drawings could be photographed directly onto the wood block. Marcus Stone's illustrations for *He Knew He Was Right* were the first drawings for Trollope in which the new process was used (although they were probably not, as F. G. Kitton reported,[6] the very first to be treated). This photo transfer process, sometimes called photoxylography, offered a number of advantages and, as will be seen, hazards as well. The artist had no longer to worry about copying or tracing his drawing onto the wood block; he could draw his original almost any size (usually somewhat larger than the intended print) because the photographic process would transmit it to the block reversed and in the dimensions required. And of course the original drawings were left perfectly intact. Fortunately, all of Stone's drawings for *He Knew He Was Right*, both full-page plates and vignettes, together with two unpublished full-page drawings, have survived and are preserved in the Arents Collection in the New York Public Library.[7] These differ from the Millais 'originals' in that they are considerably larger than the wood engravings and are drawn in black ink rather than pencil. And while there is no perfect correspondence between Stone's drawings and the printed plates (even when one takes into account the reduction in size of the latter), the likeness is striking. One would be tempted to think the plates had been made by a photographic line engraving, were it not for the most subtle variations and the signature of the engraver (here Swain). In Stone's case, then, all shaded and dark areas effected by close parallel lines and cross-hatching are the artist's own; nothing has been left to the engraver's interpretation.

While the process of photographing the drawing onto the sensitised wood block worked to advantage with Stone, the same technique led to abuses which, almost as much as the development of photographic line engraving and the half tone, hastened the end of Sixties-style wood engraving. For once photo transfer was established, the hurried or careless artist might dash off a wash drawing of any size which the engraver would then work in his own fashion. As a result, the end product was very much the engraver's: he had to supply line, interpret shadows, employ cross-hatching and parallel cuts, etc. The artist himself had abdicated much of his prerogative and responsibility. The use of wash rather than line was of course characteristic of the so-called *Graphic* school. Reproduced here for purposes of comparison with the engraved plate is Frank Holl's original wash drawing for 'Lady Laura at the Glass' (plate 81; compare 80). In this instance the engraver did fairly creditable work; in fact, the engraver has greatly improved the optics of Holl's original, which presented the viewer with a patently impossible reflected image of Lady Laura. One sees immediately that the final illustration is much more the result of the engraver's interpretation than were the plates of Millais and Stone, whose line drawings were very specifically tailored to wood engraving.

156

NOTES

INTRODUCTION

1. 'George Du Maurier', *Harper's New Monthly Magazine*, 95 (September 1897), 605. James later broadened his objection to the illustration of fiction. In his Preface to the New York Edition of *The Golden Bowl* he wrote: 'The essence of any representational work is of course to bristle with immediate images; and I, for one, should have looked much askance at the proposal . . . to graft or "grow," at whatever point, a picture by another hand on my own picture—this being always, to my sense, a lawless incident. . . . Anything that relieves responsible prose of the duty of being, while placed before us, good enough, interesting enough and, if the question be of picture, pictorial enough, above all *in itself*, does it the worst of services.' James permitted the inclusion of A. L. Coburn's photographs in the New York Edition because these 'were to seek the way . . . not to keep, or to pretend to keep, anything like dramatic step with their suggestive matter . . . the reference of [the photographs] to Novel or Tale should exactly be *not* competitive and obvious, should on the contrary plead its case with some shyness . . . [the photographs] were to remain at the most small pictures of our "set" stage with the actors left out.' (New York: Charles Scribner's Sons, 1909). pp. ix–xi.
2. *Drawing for Illustration* (London: Oxford Univ. Press, 1962), p. 35.
3. *Charles Dickens and George Cruikshank* (William Andrews Clark Memorial Library: Univ. of California, 1971), pp. 45–6.
4. *Dickens the Novelist* (London: Chatto & Windus, 1970), p. 336.
5. Henry James, 'George Du Maurier', *Partial Portraits* (London: Macmillan, 1888), pp. 344–5 (originally published as 'Du Maurier and London Society' in the *Century Magazine*, May 1883).
6. There were exceptions of course, one of which was Mrs Trollope's *Life and Adventures of Jonathan Jefferson Whitlaw*, published in three volumes in 1836 with illustrations by Auguste Hervieu.

7. Richard D. Altick, *The English Common Reader* (Chicago: Univ. of Chicago Press, 1957), p. 280.

8. For details, see Graham Pollard, 'Serial Fiction', in *New Paths in Book Collecting*, ed. John Carter (London: Constable, 1934), pp. 255ff.

9. *Novels of the Eighteen-Forties* (London: Oxford Univ. Press, 1962), p. 29. *The Old Curiosity Shop* and *Barnaby Rudge*, both illustrated, were published in the still larger imperial-octavo size of the weekly parts of *Master Humphrey's Clock*. *Hard Times* and *Great Expectations*, which appeared originally in Dickens' *Household Words* and *All the Year Round*, magazines that excluded illustrations, were published in the post-octavo size, one and three volumes respectively; *Oliver Twist* was exceptional in that, although published in the traditional three-decker format, it contained illustrations from the magazine issue.

10. Gleeson White, *English Illustration: 'The Sixties': 1855–70* (London: Constable, 1897), p. 150. White's book was republished by Kingsmead in 1970.

11. Forrest Reid, *Illustrators of the Sixties* (London: Faber & Gwyer, 1928), p. 6. For a lengthy and authoritative study of Reid's book on the occasion of its republication by Dover (1975), see Allan R. Life, ' "Poetic Naturalism" : Forrest Reid and the Illustrators of the Sixties', *Victorian Periodicals Newsletter*, 10 (June 1977), 47–68. Professor Life has also written cogently on Millais' illustrations for poetry, 'The Periodical Illustrations of John Everett Millais and their Literary Interpretation', *Victorian Periodicals Newsletter*, 9 (June 1976), 50–68.

12. Reid, p. 64.

13. Basil Gray, *The English Print* (London: Adam & Charles Black, 1937), pp. 123–6.

14. Percy Muir, *Victorian Illustrated Books* (London: B. T. Batsford, 1971), pp. 129, 134.

15. John Guille Millais, *The Life and Letters of Sir John Everett Millais* (London: Methuen, 1899), II, 493. The Dalziels said 'Millais never drew without the life'. George and Edward Dalziel, *The Brothers Dalziel: A Record* (London: Methuen, 1901), p. 42. An unpublished letter reveals Millais asking John Lane to 'try to get away so as to sit in a chair for Sir Peregrine for half an hour or so'. Letter of 11 April 1862, courtesy Yale University Library.

16. J. R. Harvey, *Victorian Novelists and Their Illustrators* (New York: N.Y.U. Press, 1971), p. 162, provides two illuminating references on this point: '[Browne] owned that he never carried a sketch-book, and

never made a memorandum from nature in his life', and Cruikshank insisted that Maclise's portrait 'represents me doing what I never did in the whole course of my life—that is *making a sketch of anyone*. All the characters which I have placed before the public are from the *brain*—after *studying and observing Nature.' Autobiographical Notes of the Life of William Bell Scott*, ed W. Minto (New York: Harper, 1892), I, 206; letter of 30 April 1873, quoted in W. Bates, *George Cruikshank, the Artist, the Humourist, and the Man* (Birmingham: Houghton & Hammond, 1878), p. 6.

JOHN EVERETT MILLAIS

1. *Letters of Dante Gabriel Rossetti*, ed. Oswald Doughty and John Robert Wahl (Oxford: Clarendon Press, 1965), I, 163.
2. Ruskin said of *Peace Concluded*: 'Titian himself could hardly head [Millais] now. This picture is as brilliant in invention as consummate in executive power; both this and "Autumn Leaves" ... will rank in future among the world's best masterpieces; and I see no limit to what the painter may hope in future to achieve. I am not sure whether he may not be destined to surpass all that has yet been done in figure-painting, as Turner did all past landscape.' *Academy Notes, 1856, The Works of John Ruskin*, ed. E. T. Cook and Alexander Wedderburn (London: George Allen, 1906), XIV, 56–7.
3. J. G. Millais, I, 343.
4. For an able defence of Millais' later works, see Mary Bennett, 'Introduction', *Millais PRB to PRA: an Exhibition Arranged by the Walker Art Gallery, Liverpool & the Royal Academy of Arts, London, January to April 1967.*
5. *Letters to Living Artists* (London: E. Mathews, 1891), pp. 16ff.

Framley Parsonage

6. *The Letters of Anthony Trollope*, ed. Bradford Allen Booth (London: Oxford Univ. Press, 1951), p. 53. References to Booth, cited as *Letters*, are given here, but texts are taken from a forthcoming new edition of Trollope's letters, edited by N. J. Hall.
7. Anthony Trollope, *Thackeray* (London: Macmillan, 1879), p. 52.

8. Anthony Trollope, *An Autobiography*, ed. Frederick Page (London: Oxford Univ. Press, 1950), p. 142. Cited hereafter as *Autobiography*.

9. In his *Thackeray*, Trollope commented on Thackeray's illustrations: 'He never learned to draw,—perhaps never could have learned. . . . But with drawing,—or rather without it,—he did wonderfully well even when he did his worst. He did illustrate his own books, and everyone knows how incorrect were his delineations. But as illustrations they were excellent. How often have I wished that characters of my own creating might be sketched as faultily, if with the same appreciation of the intended purpose. Let anyone look at the "plates," as they are called in *Vanity Fair*, and compare each with the scenes and the characters intended to be displayed, and there see whether the artist . . . has not managed to convey in the picture the exact feeling which he has described in the text' (p. 7).

10. *Letters*, p. 55.

11. *Letters*, p. 56.

12. In the same passage Trollope says of the Pre-Raphaelites: 'It is impossible to give them too much praise for the elaborate perseverance with which they have equalled the minute perfections of the masters from whom they take their inspiration. Nothing probably can exceed the painting of some of these latter-day pictures. It is, however, singular into what faults they fall as regards their subjects. . . . As a rule, no figure should be drawn in a position which it is impossible to suppose any figure should maintain . . . but the lady with the stiff back and bent neck, who looks at her flower, and is still looking from hour to hour, gives us an idea of pain without grace, and abstraction without a cause.' I am grateful to Malcolm Warner for drawing my attention to Collins' *Convent Thoughts* in this connection and for assistance at several points in this study.

13. J. G. Millais, I, 357.

14. Letter of 16 May 1860, courtesy of John Murray. The legends for about two-thirds of all of Millais' illustrations for Trollope were keyed to specific lines of dialogue or description from the text. In referring to the 'last line in the volume' Trollope was looking ahead to the three-volume book edition.

15. *Letters*, pp. 59–60.

16. White, p. 139.

17. *Modern Illustration* (London: George Bell, 1895), p. 89.

18. *Sharpe's London Magazine*, n.s. 19 (July 1861); reprinted in *Trollope:*

The Critical Heritage, ed. Donald Smalley (London: Routledge & Kegan Paul, 1969), p. 130.

19. *Saturday Review*, 11 (4 May 1861); reprinted in Smalley, p. 122.
20. *Letters*, p. 64.
21. *Letters*, p. 64.
22. *Letters*, p. 70.
23. See pp. 73–5.

Orley Farm

24. *Autobiography*, p. 167.
25. Volume in the Robert H. Taylor Collection, Princeton University Library; quoted by courtesy of Mr Taylor.
26. *Autobiography*, p. 227, and, while speaking of the success of a later novel, *Phineas Finn*, Trollope remarks that 'there was nothing in it to touch the heart like the abasement of Lady Mason when confessing her guilt to her old lover' (p. 321).
27. Millais' only lapse into melodrama was his drawing 'How can I bear it?' for Chapter lxx.
28. Richard Holt Hutton, unsigned review in the *Spectator*, 33 (11 October 1862); reprinted in Smalley, p. 146.
29. Text quoted courtesy of Mr Robert H. Taylor.
30. Letter of 11 December 1860; courtesy of the Morris L. Parrish Collection, Princeton University Library.
31. The photograph is at Orley Farm Preparatory School, Harrow; I am indebted to Michael Mason for calling this to my attention and for generously allowing me to see in typescript his provocative article, 'The Way We Look Now: Millais' Illustrations to Trollope', published in *Art History*, 1 (September 1978), 309–40.
32. Bradford A. Booth, *Anthony Trollope: Aspects of His Life and Art* (Bloomington: Univ. of Indiana Press, 1958), p. 224.

The Small House at Allington

33. *Letters*, p. 95 (misdated 1861).
34. A. O. J. Cockshut, *Anthony Trollope: A Critical Study* (1955; rpt. New York: N.Y.U. Press, 1968), pp. 151–3.
35. *Autobiography*, p. 150.

36. *Letters*, p. 131. See Michael Sadleir, *Trollope: A Commentary*, 3rd ed. (1945; rpt. London: Oxford Univ. Press, 1961), pp. 242–52.
37. *Autobiography*, p. 317.
38. Gordon N. Ray, 'Trollope at Full Length', *Huntington Library Quarterly*, 31, No. 4 (August 1968), 336.
39. See 'Artist and Engraver', p. 150ff.
40. J. G. Millais, I, 358–60. Michael Mason conjectures that Millais spent up to a week on some Trollope illustrations, although he has uncovered evidence that some of the drawings were completed very quickly: 'No. 10 of *Orley Farm* in about a day; No. 11 of *Orley Farm* in less than two days; No. 31 of *Orley Farm* in one evening; and No. 18 of *Phineas Finn* in two days.' Mason also quotes Millais' wife as saying he drew the final plate of *Framley Parsonage* three times on the block 'before being pleased'. See note 31, above.
41. In fact, at the time Trollope wrote, eighty-five. (Trollope may have counted twenty for *The Small House at Allington*, although the last two instalments were not illustrated.) Years later Millais supplied one illustration for *Kept in the Dark*, bringing his total of full-page plates for Trollope to eighty-six.
42. *Autobiography*, pp. 148–50.
43. Unsigned notice, *Eclectic Review*, ser. 8, 1 (July 1861); reprinted in Smalley, p. 128. *He Knew He Was Right* drew a similar though very hostile comment from an unidentified writer in the *British Quarterly Review*, 50 (July 1869): 'Like all Mr. Trollope's writings [*He Knew He Was Right*] is uncompromisingly realistic. . . . It is no justification of this pre-Raphaelitism that it is true to life' (reprinted in Smalley, p. 333). T. H. S. Escott recorded Trollope himself as saying: 'The art practised by Millais and myself is the effective combination of the details, which observation has collected for us from every quarter, and their fusion into an harmonious unity' and, again according to Escott, Millais 'attributed his rare success as an illustrator of Trollope's novels to the writer and artist both setting about their different work in the same way'. *Anthony Trollope* (London: John Lane, 1913), p. 203.

Can You Forgive Her?

1. Harvey, pp. 103ff. and Leavis, pp. 338ff.
2. Frederic G. Kitton, *Dickens and His Illustrators* (London: George Redway, 1899), p. 113.
3. Harvey, pp. 163ff.
4. *Autobiography*, pp. 248–9.
5. Letters to Frederic Chapman of 25 December 1863, 26 January 1864, and 31 March 1864; all in the Parrish Collection, and all summarised in Booth's edition of the *Letters*.
6. Drawing in the Arents Collection, New York Public Library. On the verso of another preliminary drawing, that for 'Baker, you must put Dandy on the bar' (Chapter xxii), Trollope complained of another inaccuracy: 'The off beast should be a mare. The two are Dandy and Flirt. The man is at Dandy's head.' Drawing in the Collection of Gordon N. Ray; words quoted in his *The Illustrator and the Book in England from 1790 to 1914* (New York: Pierpont Morgan Library, 1976), p. 79.
7. Robert M. Polhemus, *The Changing World of Anthony Trollope* (Berkeley and Los Angeles: Univ. of California Press, 1968), pp. 106–8.
8. J. G. Millais, I, 379.
9. *Letters*, p. 157.
10. Letter of 14 December 1864; from the Taylor Collection and quoted with Mr Taylor's permission.
11. This fault is repeated with even more disastrous effect in the drawing entitled ' "All right," said Burgo, as he thrust the money into his breast-pocket' (Chapter xlix).
12. Sadleir, pp. 274–5.
13. *Modern Men of Letters Honestly Criticised* (London: Hodder and Stoughton, 1870), pp. 140–1.

MARY ELLEN EDWARDS

The Claverings

1. Sadleir's transcript, property of Pickering & Chatto, London, and

quoted with their permission. It would appear that Miss Edwards was not the artist to whom Trollope, writing to Smith in March 1865, had given qualified approval as illustrator for *The Claverings* (letter in Bodleian Library; incomplete text in *Letters*, p. 162).

2. *Autobiography*, pp. 197–8.
3. Reid, p. 261.
4. Ray, 'Trollope at Full Length', p. 335.

GEORGE HOUSMAN THOMAS

The Last Chronicle of Barset

1. *Letters*, p. 187. Sadleir, p. 273, says incorrectly that Smith turned down Trollope's suggestion of asking Millais.
2. J. G. Millais, I, 284.
3. *Letters*, p. 188.
4. See note 40, under Millais, above.
5. *Letters*, p. 189.
6. *Letters*, p. 191.
7. *Autobiography*, p. 274.
8. Reid, p. 248.
9. Sadleir, p. 273.

MARCUS STONE

He Knew He Was Right

1. Kitton, p. 198.
2. Reid, p. 265.
3. Sadleir, p. 273.
4. Leavis, p. 364.
5. Letter of 30 March 1869; Trollope Papers, Bodleian.
6. *Autobiography*, pp. 321–2.
7. 'Anthony Trollope', *Partial Portraits*, 1888, reprinted in Smalley, p. 543.
8. *Autobiography*, p. 322.
9. In Sixties illustration, the first letter of the initial word of the chapter, traditionally the reason for the vignette itself, seldom formed part of

the design proper. Rather, the letter was superimposed, sometimes gracefully, sometimes clumsily, in the upper right corner of the drawing.

10. M. E. Edwards's sixteen vignettes for *The Claverings* were not included in the book edition, but those of G. H. Thomas and H. Woods for the *Last Chronicle* and the *Vicar of Bullhampton* were reproduced in the book editions.

DECADENCE

1. *Autobiography*, p. 329.
2. Unsigned notice, *Saturday Review*, 29 (4 May 1870); reprinted in Smalley, p. 336.
3. See Michael Sadleir, *Trollope: A Bibliography* (1928, rpt. London: Dawson, 1964), pp. 298–9, for a plausible explanation of the involved publication of this novel, although the mystery of the disappearance and reappearance of the illustrations remains.

    Sadleir's *Bibliography* has been an invaluable aid in making this study of Trollope's illustrators.
4. Letter of 11 April 1878; by courtesy of the Pierpont Morgan Library.
5. White, p. 93.
6. Reid, p. 216.
7. On the other hand, Ruskin had little good to say of Sixties illustration either: see *The Cestus of Aglaia*, Chapter ix, and *Ariadne Florentina*, Lecture III and Appendix.
8. Most of the illustrations for the tabloid-sized *Graphic* were considerably larger than the customary plates intended for inclusion in book editions of fiction.
9. In *Ralph the Heir* Trollope gave a fictionalised account of the Beverley election. 'Percycross and Beverley were, of course, one and the same place.' *Autobiography*, p. 343.
10. For some details on the Fildes–Fawkes mix-up, see Michael Sadleir, 'Luke Fildes', *TLS*, 5 April 1947, p. 157, and Hilda F. Finberg, *TLS*, 19 April 1947, p. 183.
11. *Letters*, p. 317.
12. Letter of 30 June 1875; by courtesy of the Pierpont Morgan Library.
13. Also to be seen in the painting are celebrities of all sorts: Gladstone, Bright, Huxley, Browning, Lady Lonsdale, Baroness Burdett-Coutts,

Mrs Langtry, Ellen Terry, Irving, Sala, Leighton, Millais, Tenniel, Du Maurier. Frith wrote that he had wished to record the 'aesthetic craze as regards dress' and 'to hit the folly of listening to self-elected critics in matters of taste, whether in dress or art'. Accordingly, Frith drew Oscar Wilde, 'a well-known apostle of the beautiful, with a herd of eager worshippers surrounding him. . . . On the left of the composition is a family of pure aesthetes absorbed in affected study of the pictures. Near them stands Anthony Trollope, whose homely figure affords a striking contrast to the eccentric forms near him.' Trollope would have appreciated the compliment. W. P. Frith, *My Autobiography and Reminiscences* (New York: Harper, 1888), p. 441.

14. 'The National Gallery', *St James's Magazine*, 2 (September, 1861), 172 and 174.

15. 'The Art Tourist', *Travelling Sketches* (London: Chapman & Hall, 1866), p. 65. Trollope makes some fairly extensive and discriminating remarks about Dutch art in 'My Tour in Holland', *Cornhill Magazine*, 6 (November 1862), 616–22.

ARTIST AND ENGRAVER

1. A similar collection, *Millais's Illustrations* (1866), contained sixteen *Orley Farm* drawings. For particulars on electrotype casts, see Harold Curwen, *Processes of Graphic Reproduction in Printing* (London: Faber and Faber, 1934), pp. 11–12.

2. A dispute in regard to drawing for the medium attended one of the most celebrated illustrations of the period, Rossetti's 'Maids of Elfen Mere' for Allingham's *Music Master*, 1855. Rossetti claimed: 'I have tried to draw all the shadow in exact lines, to which, if the engraver will only adhere, I fancy it may have a good chance.' But Rossetti's reaction to the proof was, 'That wood-block! Dalziel has made such an incredible mull of it in the cutting that it cannot possibly appear.' The Dalziels, years later, replied, 'This drawing was a remarkable example of the artist being altogether unacquainted with the necessary requirements in making a drawing on wood for the engraver's purposes. In this Rossetti made use of wash, pencil, coloured chalk, and pen and ink, producing a very nice effect, but the engraved reproduction of this many tinted drawing, reduced to the stern realities of black and white by printers' ink, failed to satisfy him.' Rossetti took his objection so far as to remove

the drawing from his copy of the book. Nearly everyone else admires the plate. *Letters of Dante Gabriel Rossetti*, I, 238, 243; *The Brothers Dalziel*, p. 86.

3. This drawing, now in a private collection, was probably that shown in the Millais Exhibition at the Grosvenor Gallery in 1886, listed as number 139 in the catalogue. I am grateful to Mr Malcolm Warner for this identification.

4. Text quoted courtesy of the Boston Museum of Fine Arts.

5. Letter of 16 September 1860, published in 'Letters from Sir John Everett Millais, Bart, P.R.A.', ed. Mary Lutyens, *The Forty-Fourth Volume of the Walpole Society: 1972–1974*, pp. 37–40.

6. Kitton, p. 201. For a detailed discussion of the process see Paul Fildes, 'Phototransfer of Drawings in Wood-block Engraving', *Journal of the Printing Historical Society*, No. 5 (1969), 87–97.

7. For an analysis of the Arents holdings in serial-novel drawings, see Hellmut Lehmann-Haupt, 'English Illustrators in the Collection of George Arents', *The Colophon*, New Graphic Series, No. 4, 1 (January 1940), n.p. [341–64].

INDEX

INDEX

All references are to page numbers. Plates are designated by page numbers in square brackets